Spirit in Three Heart Songs

Awaken - Heal - Expand

Transcribed by L.M. Reed
Illustrated and designed by Gracie Walsh

DEDICATION

Although it often seems like we are on the road alone, in reality many surround us to provide encouragement with loving hands and open hearts.

Special thanks to Debbie DeRusha and Healing Inspirations for providing the spark and safe space that lit the way.

Heartfelt appreciation to my angel friends Michele and Linda who guided the way to all messages helpful and hopeful.

And to my eternal love, Dave, who has meandered with me through the cosmos, holding my hand with steadfast love and devotion.

And of course, infinite gratitude to spirit for sharing these messages with me. They merely asked me to listen, write and share. I sit in awe of their words and thank them for trusting my hands to deliver them to others in search of healing light.

Greetings

This quest began with an intuitive development class involving the Akashic records. The instructor walked us through a meditation to the doorstep of the records. Reading one, *Welcome*, is the outcome of the first step in this journey. The rest are one small human's efforts to understand existence as we know it. The readings were gifts offered to me for my own soul development. I was asked to place them into the stream for other seekers who might benefit from them, so I transcribed them faithfully over time.

These readings attempt to convey through just one human means—words—the vast connection of all in body and spirit with the divine, in messages they have called Heart Songs. These words describe the spirit truth that emanates from each heart center as threads of energy connected to all other beings.

These messages came in three separate books to show three phases of spiritual development, although readers will see overlap and cross-referencing of main ideas in all three parts. Spirit often used metaphors (earthly comparisons) and paradoxes (opposites that are true) to describe the cosmic reveries intended to heal wounds and expand growth. An awakened mind and heart can understand that contradictions really aren't opposites. They are just many facets of one whole that are neither conflicts nor limits. Paradox allows us to see and accept all 'impossible' contradictions that present as confusing, false choices and restrict our sight.

Heart Song 1, *Awaken*, explains how we long to understand our authentic soul and our own connection to the divine. It encourages us see with new eyes to understand the intricacies of the human-spirit-divine relationship. To awaken we must first see.

Heart Song 2, *Heal*, encourages us to delve deeply into our hearts to understand the spiritual purpose of human pain in order to heal ego wounds that inhibit spiritual development. Healing requires us to open-heartedly embrace the difficulties inherent in life, while accepting self as both flawed and perfect as is.

Heart Song 3, *Expand*, shifts our gaze from in to out to encourage us to live an authentic, soul-fulfilling life as spirit in body. Once dark corners are exposed to light, it is possible to live our energy fully and assume the role of co-creators in our destiny. This requires us to understand the narrative we have written in the past and how we can create a new narrative more satisfying to our true nature. Once aware and healed, we can use our open heart and hands to craft our own spirit truth daily.

It is with a most earnest heart that I wish you well on your journey of healing and expansion. I hope you find some comforting nugget of truth in these messages that helps you progress in your own search for an illuminated and loving life.

L. M. Reed

Don't sleep on the journey. Don't pull down the shades.
Being present is not a cliché.
It is an awakening of the spirit.

CONTENTS

Heart Song 1- Awaken

Welcome
Reading 1

It is a tale of divine and earthly connection played out over eons on the vast stage of the universe.

Entry into the universal space began with a bright, blinding light, followed by a brilliantly lit fog.

Eventually the fog cleared and I was standing in the middle of a circular, wall-less structure. Stars ringed the space and I knew I was viewing the entire universe. It was breathtaking.

There were unseen beings around me. They said, "Welcome. We have been waiting to see you again."

One older man emerged to greet me. I knew him, but I didn't, if such a thing is possible. He hugged me and I knew I was safe. He said, "There is no hurry. We are glad you found us. There is a lot to discover. Take your time. Looking around is enough for now. Just enjoy the place." *I was left to explore the circular structure, with its spectacular view of the vast space in the universe.*

I began to puzzle about the presence of a library, but just sensed it and somehow the man presented me with a book that he said held my story. I asked who recorded it and he said, "You do!" *very emphatically.*

I remember laughing and asking how accurate it could be if I was writing my own story. He said, "You write beyond any earthly constrictions that blind you."

I was so excited I hugged the book. MY STORY WAS IN HERE!! I was reminded that there was no hurry and as I hugged it, I felt its warm glow enter my heart.

Then the instructor called us back and I must admit, I was a little annoyed at having to leave.

Return visit—same session

I entered the structure again and they all said, "You're back!"

Everyone was going on about their business. I was just wandering among them. I asked them, "What are you doing?" *They said,* "Living—in a way. Thinking. Learning. Knowing. Sharing. Loving."

My book appeared. I moved it around in my hands as it changed colors and shapes. Light pulsed from the pages.

I was told the book wasn't a real book and the story wouldn't be told in words. These are just compiled ideas. Recorded experiences. A rich history. The book is just a metaphor, so you can envision it. It is a compilation of residual energy—past imprints of life experiences. It is your life told in energy that is beyond human comprehension. It is a tale of divine and earthly connection played out over eons on the vast stage of the universe.

Then she called us back and the message was over.

Discovery
Reading 2

Your story will be written now and into the eons.

Floating through air, seeing fog, progressing toward it. Not light like last time I arrived but not seeing anyone. Seems a bit gray today. A figure comes out a little slowly, not with welcoming as before. "You are heavy today, weighed down by the world. This will make it hard for you to see."

In truth, all is not light where we are. We carry with us residual feeling of humans, although for the most part, our bodies are behind us, but our concerns for the world are not. We will always feel the weight of sorrow and reflect the feeling of man because we are explicitly tied together and can't divorce ourselves. Ego dominates us there and while we carry pieces of light recollections with us, here is the reverse. We carry mostly light, but ego does not abandon us, so we keep empathy with those suffering from earthly concerns. If we got rid of them completely, how would we remember how to feel what you feel?

We are glad you are undertaking this endeavor. All this searching will never come to an end, but you have always asked the questions yearning in your soul and now you shall be given a glimpse of the answers. But know they are limited by your body and ego, and your understanding of the world is through a narrow lens. If you can accept that, then you're welcome to hear what we have to say without worrying about the scope of your understanding.

Do you have any idea what I should be doing with this information?

For now, just learn. Take your soul as you have always imagined it and enrich it. Make it glow with our fire. Make it safe in our knowledge. Become evolved on a higher plane.

Clearly that is why you have come here full of questions. You have demanded answers your whole life, now can you accept that about yourself? You have been given knowledge that something different exists. Now it is time to see what that difference is—why you have been suffering with the knowledge that something is not right. It is just beyond your grasp. Well, time for you to try to grasp the immensity of it and we shall see where that takes you. Who knows? We have a suspicion, but are you ready for that now? Perhaps your purpose on the earth right now is to develop your understanding of the connection between the divine and earthly. Nothing more may be required at this time.

You will see perhaps that those worries can be transcended through soul light and darkness can be banished. Maybe your purpose is just a higher you and not a higher place to spread divine destiny. The truth may come to you as you learn more but may not be the reason for you to join us now. Can you accept that?

Yes, I can. I would settle, though I do not like the word settle because it means I have not.

No. Change the 'settle' to 'accept'. That is the question I asked you! Your story resides here and visiting us enriches it, but maybe you aren't meant to be a Mother Theresa. See? Perhaps you are supposed to be better, more soul developed. The real purpose of life journeys on. You are worried about not learning enough about your story. You are always in such a hurry, so demanding!

Life lesson for you, dear one. There is no hurry. Time stretches on. Your story will be written now and into the eons. See that universe? It is timeless. Most of your dark concerns are about events in time, suspended in time, happening in a moment of time. Perhaps we want you to know that time is a human construct based on limitation. It is the way we decided to play out your visits on earth. Eventually your earthly visits will be seen as mere specks of experience in a continuum of non-earthly experiences.

See the dot that is out there? See the rest of it stretching out behind you and before you? Perspective, dear one, is so very important. Here you have come down into the world to feel uncomfortable, unfit, poorly constructed in your current time and place. It makes you examine the idea of true value and self regardless of momentary universe placement. Yes, you are suffering a bit now the shoe does not fit well. Human existence is a struggle for you and maybe you needed to be reminded of its constrictions—a bit too callous to humans. Perhaps you forgot what it feels like to straddle both.

I can't wait to read my story.

Yes, you can and you will. We are not running a race here. We are taking a stroll and looking at the leaves and the beauty of the energy that pulses in them, the connection we have to them and to each other regardless of soul force development. Are you ready to take a stroll? Are you ready to take a walk with me?

First, slow down. You are making me tired! Such a hurry! Breathe. Feel and enjoy love. Know we are here. Come and visit. We will take a walk periodically and chat. Bye for now, loved one.

Can I just wander a moment to see what I can see?

Certainly. Stay for a bit. Look around. It is your home after all.

It seems darker today. The book appears. I stroke its pages—no name on front. Many names have lived this soul. See light from pages. Eventually the book disappears and I could see the contents in their real form: experiences, blips, emotions, energy imprints. I cannot tell organization, just all together at center is solid, condensation of soul. Again, just physical manifestation, more like dense black hole of living energy that is me. Mine. Red, black—experiences around drawn by a gravity of sorts held together by central force of the soul. Just add to it with experience, insight, growth. Infinite in its capacity. Trying to touch it. Energizing. What power! Hold it in my hands. Feel it flow through me. Love the feeling! Power, safety, something transcendent. I can see its connection to divine and all other things.

We are indeed all connected to universe and each other and divine power. We are not the owners of that, but the beneficiaries of the power. We can choose to harness and acknowledge and develop it. We will all see it eventually but can access it while still here. You are one who can choose to do that if you want.

Yes, I do very much. Don't let me forget.

You can't stay here all day. It would exhaust you. Little bites of cake. You need to ponder and translate. Good luck.

Open
Reading 3

Embrace your lessons. Isn't that enough for today?

Hello. Welcome back. You keep coming, so we have much to share. You will take your time and unfold the truth as you can see and understand it. You do not need to see the vastness, but if it helps you, we will use it as backdrop to truth, to put forth a semblance of scope to ease your mind of restrictions. Open up, open up, open up to truth and it will be solace for you.

I am not sure how much I have to offer in terms of your worldly struggles, but I can link you to the greatness that lies here. Look around. Isn't it magnificent? We reside here in vastness of depth, distance, understanding. Just look. Take it all in. Feel it. It awaits you and your limited understanding.

I cannot give you all the answers of why humans behave as they do. All the souls you know have earth-bound problems. To develop, the soul needs to struggle with complexity and certainly human emotion provides that. How can we develop here when it is so vast and we have greater insight? Where is the challenge? Doesn't growth come from challenge in many cases?

The only problem is people do not have any reverse sight into what happens here when they are there, so they have the tiniest pinprick of light to illuminate their experience. Well, they could, but it isn't the norm. Most people are mired in their earthiness and cannot escape it long enough to see beyond the wall. See, no walls here to restrict. Bodily walls. Environmental walls. Just free souls and yet how to grow? Challenge is how to grow, so we come back to take on a host of issues that will enrich our soul lives and struggle away for an earthly life.

It might end early because we are done or have made enough progress. We might end it because the path we have chosen is too fraught with despair to continue, so we will try again. And yet, we keep trying and growing and expanding ourselves in the truest nature available, which brings us closer to the divine. We seek to think about that divine state. That is why we leave here. That is why we live there. Humanity is plagued by small natures, which explains evil, darkness, prejudice and hate. We come down there to work through these, but as human we have oh, so limited vision. How to see that which is so much bigger than the small peephole available to human eyes? We come back and work it out.

For now, you need to know why you are there. You used to think it was to make a large impact on the world. Mostly it is to work through your own soul issues and hold out a hand to others, so others can learn theirs. Why do suppose you became a teacher? Why so many questions? You are ready to know more than others, which makes you more responsible for the holding out of a hand to help them along, so yes, you are there for that purpose but on a smaller scale than once imagined. Perhaps if a bigger scale is called for it will appear.

Souls are constantly redefining their paths there and here, so do not be surprised if something shifts and opportunity appears. Part of your soul search is to find opportunity for development. Believe me it presents itself when you are ready to accept it. That peephole just isn't wide enough sometimes, but you are working right now to open the peephole wider both in and out. You have a window installed in your soul, but until now the opening appears at times and you peer in. Well, that is your challenge. How much to grow? How much to see? How much to learn this time?

Okay, enough. Just wander about. Consider the vast surround. Feel the immensity. Appreciate your soul place here. Feel how comfortable it is. Maybe you can fit here better. Maybe your hands will be able to reach out more. Heart will expand wider. Embrace the divine that creates and surrounds us. Our teacher. You are a student made teacher. Now maybe you can understand more what you need to do as student to the divine. Better now that you have experienced teaching.

Feel the hands grasp. Energy flow. Connection of love and learning. Heat driving us towards light, banishing darkness; thriving, learning, seeking peace. Embrace your lessons. Isn't that enough for today?

Yes, but it feels so full, I don't want to leave.

Come back. It is yours to feel and take back. It is yours here and there in you.

Peering over edge of structure. How vast. How beautiful. How powerful. I could jump and I would be safe. I step off edge into universe and was able to walk out away from structure. Walking on air. Impossible to describe the embrace of the feeling. Open arms. Energy flow. Amazing.

Take this back with you.

Awareness
Reading 4

Enjoy the sweetness of life. Preciously golden, as is your soul, in all of it.

We have had trouble holding back all those thoughts flooding you. Be careful to protect self from constant flow of information. Empowering, yes. Always productive, no.

We see you coming to join us again! Welcome to our plane. We feel fuller when you are here and embrace your presence into our loving arms. You belong here in a way you do not always belong there, so bask in it for now. We all belong here—lucky you to see it before others. Gazing around, can't you see it? Beauty. Power. Life pulsing through the universe! You are but a small dot in it, but within you small dot of understanding swells. All dots within dots—connected to within and without. Make a pause on questioning while here. Just listen, absorb. Think later. Bask now. Enjoy now. Be at peace now.

You wonder about your place here, your place there. We all have a place in the universe. Tangible form there, spiritual form here. One swells within the other, reversing itself depending on where you are at the moment. God has placed in all beings powers of light, but challenges of dark. Challenge is really to harness both to see connection between and beyond.

Connection is the theme of your life and all the lives of people and beings. People you are with when there. Souls you are with when here. Both times, beings are the same, just different shape, form, name, time. All those earthly connections linked together in a stream of never-ending energy. Not a timeline per se, but a continuation of development, different pieces of peace. I know you love words, so we shall play. They, too, are human construct to make sense possible. In soul form, though, not always necessary, just as not always necessary there. So many realities words fall short of describing, just as bodies of humans do as well. Such greatness tempered with such flaws—life!

Your awareness this time rests on the realization that connections exist where you have always felt disconnection, so pain is generated from that. Not sure you are ready to embrace that idea yet, but it is coming. You already feel and see the power of the universe as a warm energy exuding from a part of you into the world. Please see it as healing wounds that nothing else can heal—the wounds of humanity in yourself.

First, you can through recognition of soul force, envision soul, see the patchwork of energy forces. We are everywhere in that form. Be ready to embrace ideas beyond human comprehension. Just see things that you can't see through eyes, feel things beyond mind and heart. Take with you power of forces beyond the imaginable. Why do you always see this as necessary for change? Enlightenment doesn't require great change to spread it. It requires seeing beyond the visible, feeling beyond the emotional and understanding beyond the comprehensible. Again, I urge you to walk around and take stock here. I know it feels like home to you. Safe. You wanted to step off into the universe.

I do it. I walk over to the ends of the structure constructed to help me understand the place. I look over the edge. Stepping off is such a risk, but I am confident I can do it. I take one step, then another and I enter light and darkness at once. It is one. My feet are supported, but I am without my feet. In soul form, so no feet needed. Suspended in energy. Draped in energy. Cocooned in energy. Incomprehensibly amazing. Around me all the energy of other souls, one, yet separate—pulsing with what? Life force, energy. Connection is there whether we see it or not. We are all one life force with different forms to take us there.

I told you to enjoy the moment of energy submersion. You really are seeing and feeling ways not entirely human. All the soul force around you is in different forms. You have known many of them. The ones you think you know now, you have only known a short time by that name. Maybe you have known others. There is no one connection here and there.

We welcome your visits as you provide us with reminders of humanity's limits and struggles. Reminders about why we go there and how to grow here without real struggle to bring about change. As a human, you have been given a glimpse of the otherworldly to help understand the worldly life you lead connected to others in ways you do not, cannot, understand. Come back when you wish. We await your arrival. Chat and walk with us, but don't forget the spectacular nature of love and life there. You will be tempted to think that life here is better because human emotional pain is lessened.

Remember. Not gone here. Lessened. But be afraid to miss the spectacular nature of the world there. Breathe the fresh air. Listen to birds. Feel the grass under your toes. Revel in the love of all you know. Since it is harder there, it is also more dear. Cherish the opportunity and open to bring it to fruition. Such a gift to be able to see benefits of here and there at same time. Not all get that chance! Something to relish there. Something to look forward to here. Lucky you.

Farewell. Enjoy the sweetness of life. Preciously golden, as is your soul, in all of it. Farewell.

Connection
Reading 5

Here it is. Be yourself.

Wandering through gray. Looking. Staying open. Burst onto universe. Ah! So, breathtaking. Hard to imagine or describe. Want to be there, not just imagining being there.

Hello, dear one. Welcome back. We are so happy to see you again. We welcome you here to share gifts of insight and understanding. You may not feel it. I suspect you do. That your confidence in yourself and us is growing. We are here to lead you to your true nature as a whole human and spirit as you merge in harmony to one. Although all your questions will not be answered here, you will see light you have never seen and feel peace you have never known. So, what is your mission today?

How do I find my place in the world or do I make a place where I am and live with disconnect?

Today's topic—connection.

You have always known that the jigsaw puzzle of your life left you little room for comfortable fit. View all as oddly shaped pieces. Perhaps you are the elusive piece, misplaced outside the box or perhaps just a piece like everyone else. Who is to say? But that doesn't help your current situation, now does it?

Relationships. You have been wandering the earth for people like you and so far, have not found many. You discuss earthly things with those you meet, but clearly that is not important to your essence. You are seeking something else, so they don't know what to say or what to do.

Here it is. Be yourself. How could people find you before if you were pretending to be something else? You expected people to accept you for what you were, but were you really presenting you? In some ways, your whole life has been one to adapt, appease, fit in the puzzle to complete the puzzle. What you really want is to fit in the puzzle. You are asking something of people they cannot do as they fit in snugly. Make room for the odd shaped piece—not their thing. Perhaps accepting your life outside the puzzle is okay. Just be your own piece and say your own truth.

Let's talk about the spirit within you. You are a child of God as are all those around you, so why the disconnect? Some people are children of God, but humanness dominates them. Earthly concerns overwhelm them. They see nothing about the light within them, thus hatred, racism, power, greed, unfortunate, but true. They came here to seek enlightenment as we all do, but it is not for them this time—or maybe something will cause a crack in the mirror and they will see more than they did before.

As spirit, your job is not to crack the mirror. Open the window. It is to understand what is playing out in the tableau before you—both on earth and in spirit. Seeing is not as easy as you might think, especially while on earth. Can you not see that?

HA! You have said there is a window between you and others on earth and between you and understanding spirit. Perhaps your challenge now is to watch that window melt and cope with the fact you can reach into both worlds with more understanding. Imagine yourself perched in a window with arms outstretched in both directions—into the garden of humanity and into the vast space of spirit. What an unusual place to be. What a fabulous opportunity for you to grow and develop. Use your humanity to understand spirit.

Fortunate. How can that make you a problem? What is the problem? You can live in both. Don't be intolerant of those who do not see or cannot bridge the expanse of knowledge. Reaching into both worlds should not ever be seen as a problem. It is a gift and we urge you to see it as such. Connection? You are struggling with this connection to both worlds, so as you become less of a problem in spirit, more of a problem in humanity. Seeing beyond is not a problem. Learning to shape it and grow from it as your human restrictions exert themselves can be. Imagine yourself as fitting in the puzzle not as a piece, but as a speck of energy that engulfs and unites all of life. How can that not be a wonderful place to be? Why is that pain? Joy in energy! Joy in self! Joy in connection to divine!

Patience with humanity. Patience with heartache. Joy in humanity and the ability it offers you to grow! To understand why you are here. Connection is an interesting worry. How to be so connected and so disconnected? Managing that is indeed a challenge. It is the place you have always been, but as the glass melts it is time to seize power from it and recognize the good it can do for you and all others. Learning measured connection—one inch to the right of yourself as observer. Continue to bask in glow of energy that is in you as divine connection gift. The gift of seeing. Gift of knowing. Gift of feeling that much bigger than yourself.

How is this connection a problem? You know you were talking about problems with early connections—not really the problem you perceive through pain. Just is. You do not have a place in the puzzle. Perhaps. Is that so bad? Much to consider. Think about this.

Walk around your place and feel the energy. Enjoy the vastness. We shall be here for you again. We love you. Love yourself as you are part of the universe and deserving of all good that comes from it.

The original circular structure appears, but then disappears. It is having trouble sustaining itself.

Remember, it is an artificial construct. There is no place like that you imagined. We showed you in response to your desire, your human need to see for yourself. Now you know there is no such place. It is just vast space and you are in it, one with it. Included, nestled in a much bigger puzzle with no sharp edges and delineating lines, just swaddled in peace and comfort and love with no space between spirits. You can read your story without a book in your hands. Isn't that what we just discussed? The story of you on earth at this time and place. How much do you think you can grasp at once? You still are human after all. Let it go for now.

Seeing
Reading 6

What is that knot?

We will start with place again. We want you to see the physical manifestation of location (vast celestial library). Feel its power. This is not you. All that is stored in these books and not-books, swirls of energy that make up you and all others and that merge with infinite source that is bigger than you. However, that being said, you have only one brain to filter it. Your humanity is filter screen. How else? This makes message imperfect at best. Yes, it is true—coming from both infinite and you. Can't you see the two are one? You want to know if you are creating this in a whirl of desires. If this is coming from your imagination, hopes, dreams. That is a possibility, but what about what you feel and know to be true? Brains believe what they want to believe, often in spite of clear evidence or not so clear evidence; otherwise, humanity suffers from filter by design. Struggle inherent in your experience. Have to struggle to learn, so given imperfect filters.

Challenge is to see—merely to see. Wade through the filters. Move hands through the mud to clear vision. What can you see past your nose? What can you see when peering into dark night? Light does exist in pinpricks. In elusive flashes. Once in a while people catch the gaze of light and feel its warmth and know that this is true (and it is), but then it goes away and we are in mud once again.

So why come here? It is your attempt to wade through mud. Push darkness aside and seek further to know truth, but then you return with all your doubts and darkness. Even if most of your life is filtered through a human lens, can't you believe there is something else around you at all times? You just can't see it with your human eyes. Do not be afraid to let yourself be here. Keep peering into the darkness. What difference does it make if at one time or another you are seeing, hearing spirit or casting doubt and blocking as human? All originates in your brain. You just have to believe (or not) that your brain's consciousness extends beyond the darkness of humanity and meets the infinite in a graceful dance you do not always appreciate. Do you really want to cut this off in fear that your brain may be playing tricks? That your reality here is not true?

Envision your brain as the computer board that processes the true information. You must accept that it may not be electricity powering it. Maybe it is indeed power, but not that which is man-made. Power is the source of this. Do you believe in otherworldly power or not? That is your decision. Yes, this comes from your brain, but where originally? Theory when you die—all that you see is merely dying brain cells. Or is it bigger? We tell you yes, but it is up to you to decide how much of that is real in your experience and how much is biology and factual brain orientation. Brain/spirit— yes. Both true. Your desire to know indicates brain theory. You are envisioning brain and soul window. See how the energy comes into you and enters the filter of human experience. Do with that image what you will. Find comfort or discouragement. Both inherent in humanity.

I look around the circular structure and am struck by the vast expanse of reality. Yes, that I know is a human construct, a beautiful one, but human nonetheless. When I step off, I enter the reality of merging spirit and brain. The feeling is surges of power and energy. It does not feel human. As I can feel my own energy and see connection of energy to all those around me, I feel almost as though beautiful construct is not true figment of human brain. Must make sense of the (non)sensical. Lovely word. Should look it up. Perhaps what I am doing is indeed (non)sensical, but not as in nonsense—as in no sense—beyond senses.

When you come to see us, reside here and we will continue to guide you through the mud. Clear your eyes a bit. Comfort you with understanding. That which you crave more than anything—connection, peace, understanding . . . but not at brain level, at spirit level. Keep both in mind as you weigh our input.

What to do next? I am trying to stay open, but what does that mean? How to stay open to spirit and destiny with no sense of direction?

Again, you try to impose human parameters on bigger ideas. You want to be the one who controls, sees, interprets, understands and follows direction. How open is that? Be careful your residual restlessness does not block your vision. We have told you to relax, look around, explore. Try (non)sensical activities. Feel the cushion of energy around as you do. Self-comfort. Connection. Purpose comes from that. Not before that. Live your life. Purpose stems from that. Opportunity comes from living life.

We can discuss this more but think about it first. What is that knot? As you do, what is the source of that entanglement and deep unhappiness? With what? Certainly not embracing, open. Challenge again. Open heart. You hear that every time and you remain heart-closed and tight and worried. Examine that knot. Hard fisted. Lump of unhappiness. Did you think the golden gates would just open and your perfect opportunity would just apparate in front of you? Hmm...We shall talk of this next time.

We have said enough. Feel the lack of boundaries. Hold your story in your hands. Listen. Watch. Peer into the darkness. Move the mud away from your eyes. Live here and there.

Heart
Reading 7

If your heart remains tightly closed, it will go nowhere.

Hello dear one. Welcome today. Are you ready with open heart? I know that is your biggest challenge—open heart. We shall try to pry it open a bit. Without openness, you cannot proceed. Wide open vision. Look around you. Seeing not so important. Feeling crucial. Can you feel my message today? That is how you are going to access us more fully. We understand the need to see, visualize, but we are a feeling lot. Energy is a feeling activity. Begin to do that and you shall learn more, see more, develop more.

Envision heart center. Valentine's Day appropriate, but just a little, ha! I know you can feel people there. Can you feel them here?

The heart swells with the energy of masses, merged with my energy, overwhelmingly powerful.

Just bask. Stop the words.

I sit in blackness and realize I am not separate. At first, I feel people, spirits as separate entities, but not after a while. A pool of energy ignites all, unites all.

First, what to do with this? Pure joy is yours if you choose to tap into the divine. That should be sufficient, but we know it won't be as you are not one to accept, but that should become the very baseline of your life. It is there. You are in it. Focus on the positive power of good in the universe. The divine overwhelms. Evil exists there and residual regret here as we puzzle how to progress to the divine, but powerful energy governs all and you are now aware that you are part of it.

For now, just become self-aware. Tap into power. Why must you always be fretting about next step? Next step is to feel, understand, enjoy, appreciate, connect, develop. If it goes no further, so what? So farther ahead than you were. Can be reservoir of strength when earthly worries overcome you. Make the trip back to your chair in the universe. It will remain there for your respite.

Eventually you will be lead to other paths or shall we say create other paths? We can hold up the tableau of possibilities. Your choices will lead you forward, either here or there. Not sure which yet. You seem puzzled. What do with this information. Must you share? It is for you. Compulsion to share will come later with understanding and maybe opportunity as well. Why do you need to know today? Well, spelling doesn't matter, so stop worrying. Listen to us. Sit in your chair and bask. Let the energy and messages flow.

Today is a precious day. Every day is a precious day. Cold makes you alive. Plants make you alive. God gives you energy life—life here and there. Power makes you alive.

Despair is human and kills life force, so you should try to overcome that. Perhaps today's lesson is to focus. Focus on that which makes you strong. You are so just a baby, just learning.

The fact you have been offered this glimpse is a gift and you must appreciate that and make good use of it in your life and not just for your own happiness. You can't let that spread good into the world until it takes firm root in you. No second guessing. Confidence in your place in the universe will bring you great joy and make it possible to use the force for good in ways yet unforeseen.

For now, it is a tight circle centered in your heart, but if your heart remains tightly closed, it will go nowhere. You will feel it on occasion and bask in it, but you will never be able to use it properly unless it becomes your baseline view of the world. You carry it with you most of the time, an open, powerful heart, big enough to share rather than the kernel of light you possess now. Your choice is to nurture, expand and share, or harbor it tightly and extinguish it by dwelling in dark, painful, fearful places. What a shame that would be, but your choice. Your heart.

You can do it now or you can try it again next time, but this life would be far more vivid if you choose to do it now. You have light and love to nurture, have been given the luxury of time, insight, resources to fan the flame and live an exceptional life. Small little girl to open hearted woman. Take her by the hand. The flame has been with you always, but shrouded, protected, wounded. Time to consider taking off the shroud and living in love's light. It will give you nourishment beyond your wildest dreams. Happiness of a divine sort. Holy assurance of connection and worth. If you are strong enough to overcome the chains you have placed on your spirit, you must be the one to remove them. We cannot do that for you. The shroud keeps you in darkness. Smile on your heart and open it to the energy offered by the divine and universal power shall reside in you. Later you can use that in the world, but not yet. You aren't sure enough.

You have always longed to do great things. Maybe you will. Maybe your greatness lies in being able to access us and respond and develop in spirit gift to you. Insight into that feeling unlike any others. Keep reading. Keep visiting us. Keep that flame in your mind's eye, and your heart's hopes and dreams, and we will take you into our loving arms and show you the way.

Enjoy for a moment before returning. You will see (feel) what we mean.

I float in a sea of energy and hold out my hands. They are alight with gorgeous sparks of vivid white blue light. I can feel everyone and everything around me. Cosmic embrace. Peace. Freedom. Safety. Love. How divine. Literally I have just discovered my hands can be used to access this. Reading energy flows through my hands. Must remember that.

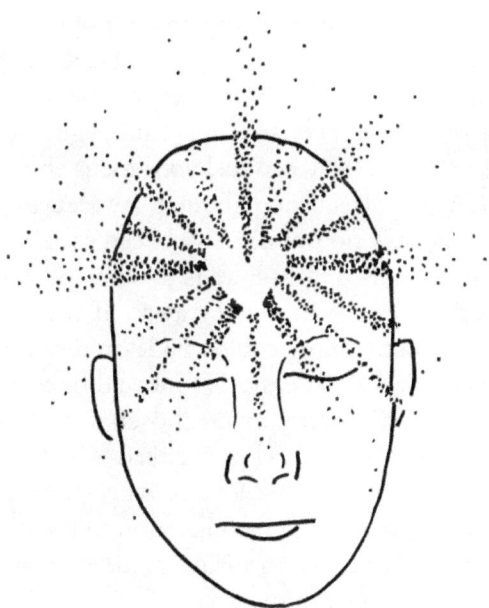

Purpose
Reading 8

The path of energy does not stretch out before you prewritten.

Thank you for coming back. I know you are skeptical. Bear with us. You know we are here to share the truth of life lived there and life growing after. Such a ribbon! You are beginning to see the events as they unwind in an endless stream of life pulsing through the universe. The expanse and the influence are vast. You are beginning to put your fingertips on them and feel energy pulsing. Hands important tools for feeling, sensing. You have always known your hands were sensitive, but how so? Feel truth, light, energy, pulse through endlessly. We can feel your focus shifting from there to here. Not really shifting, though. Awareness just of what does exist. Really no boundary between realms. Just the mind shutting doors, creating walls to allow people to function in worldly without too much awe. If you knew truth about vast expanse, how could you learn messy lessons of humans? It would be too easy. You would be too unconcerned. You have pretty much chosen to feel pain to trigger growth. Love and pain closely linked—on both sides of coin. Learning pain can cause love or hate. Lesson in that. Always struggle to learn ultimate connection to the divine, which is love; a slow, endless, torturous ramble toward uniting with the divine power of love.

Of course, some cling to hate, which is really brainchild of fear. It causes people to forget ultimate goal—struggle toward love and if you embrace hate you have taken detour and will not make it to destination. Try again. Chutes and ladders for earthly analogy.

So, beware of fear. It will take you down paths that hurt the soul, block its growth. You have been feeling surges of life. Love flows through you in unlikely places. Let it wash over you like balm. It is healing. Bask in it like the sun that is given you to enlighten. It engulfs your soul and provides a path through darkness and toward the light of God's love.

So, what is your purpose here on earth?

Well, individual light in yourself. How you have struggled with love and closed heart! You have come through fire on many occasions and always found way to pinprick of light. Does not make you enlightened, but know you are on the right path. Pinprick is small vision of what is possible. How overwhelming to think of that writ large. Must ready your mind for envisioning that possibility. Too much for human to grasp at once! Think of light gradually arriving at dawn. That is your soul gaining power, love and insight. Don't forget darkness happens too; balance in all things. It is tremendous, vivid feeling of both light and dark. Both exist in stream with gradual dawn your goal of enlightenment.

What for others? You are doing that. Only need to raise awareness of role you are filling. Importance of your role in providing support. Such a rock! Planning, implementing, making life flow for those who need it in your circle. Bigger circle. Some people seek enlightenment, some don't seem to want it. Your mistake comes when you try to force that which you see on people who have not sought your insight. You feel it is best to speak up and offer, but they didn't want or need it, so what is purpose of forcing it? See how it makes you out of place and angers some who prefer to see life on own path? So what if you see? Unless sought, the insight is not for you to offer. If the time is right for it, they will ask. If not, just sit back and enjoy the fact you can see it differently and hone your own ability to perceive. Just connect to their path of energy, which really isn't different from your own.

To what end? Why should you develop this? Who knows? The path of energy does not stretch out before you prewritten. It is a path that is free of energy imprints and those are embedded, scripted by your choices, so it remains to be seen what you will do with this. The script is not written. Insight comes, use comes later. Since when did you get an education and know where it would take you? Why did you think this was different? Could you have anticipated teaching career while learning? It will just enable things to happen on a personal level. You will become better at feeling energy with others. Sometimes it will come in handy. Sometimes they will ask and maybe sometimes it will be valued by others. Maybe not, though. We shall see, won't we?

Try to stay pure in your pursuit. We will guide you where this is taking you. Baby steps. What do you think now that you are seeing a broader landscape? Isn't it fabulous?

I decide to just sit back and look around the space. It is dark, but sparks of lights, hologram images, teem through the air as life pulses throughout the universe. I am watching life lived in real time. How interesting! I am alone in my sea of observation yet surrounded by infinite dots of energy living their lives. This is the gift! I can see it. I can become better at feeling it. I can use it. Maybe it works out that way. For now, just bask in greatness, hive of life moving. Interesting. Not really a forward or back, so how does time fit into this? I have always assumed there is movement forward, but it appears not. Just is. More like treading water.

Does light grow where it is instead? Hmmm. How do soul clusters work, exactly? Another puzzle. Time. Souls. How to come together on a finite path for personal growth, then return to timeless state? Interesting. Pause. Floating. Aware. Using hands to reach out. Sparks again. I will try this on earth to see what happens. Don't want to leave but must. Too much to process at once. Take snapshot of this vision for later. Peace.

So, a peek behind the curtain. What say you to its vast scope beyond human comprehension?

What a gift! Thank you. I will process and be back for more.

Limits
Reading 9

Pain limits a quiet revolution in heart.

Welcome, dear one. It is good to see you again. Time to put aside your earthly concerns and let us flow in. You need to set aside those concerns that trouble you and think beyond concerns there to think about life here and how it illuminates you and provides you with love.

Get in right mind to hear. See the life of the universe bubble with light around you. Floor. Ceiling. Ribbon of time disappeared and here you float. Look around. Stunning.

Consider all those you live with now. What role do they play? Who are they in your life? What challenges do they present? Lessons one and all. Do not wait until the deathbed to figure out while life tock ticks away. No failed opportunities—as yet. Perhaps examination of each. Why did you come there together? What lessons await you? How does love expand into those hearts and join you together? What role plays the struggle and how to get beyond it to learn and find love?

Love and appreciate them all for what they offer you in your journey. If they present struggle, see their souls and try to link spirit. That will guide your growth there and here.

Look around the universe to see the energy beyond the two levels you think you can accept now. Limits. Again limits. Your time limits. Your vision limits. Your human form limits you.

Move beyond earthly and spirit limits to see vast expanse of energy possibility.

Forgiveness there is important because expectations limit, restrict vision, inhibit expansive growth. Seek higher thoughts. Bigger heart. More understanding. Life insight. Life in all its forms, on all its levels. Expansion key right now. Break expectations, walls. Pain limits a quiet revolution in heart. It will open you to expansion with no other goal in mind. Seek understanding whole heartedly. Raise the flag of knowing. Stake a claim to love and freedom of spirit for its own sake and nothing more. We are ending here. This is plenty. Think. Feel. Love. Open precious gift of insight to guide path. Enjoy and value it.

The place can flood with light if enlightened. Seek it. Light is love. It is right. It is divine.

Choice
Reading 10

Can you accept that it just is?

We sense a great block between us now. Your reluctance speaks volumes of fear. We can feel you repelling us at every turn. Take a moment and try to open your mind before we continue. You must truly want to hear, or our time will be wasted.

I am back at the round room surrounded by the universe, in the library. I can see the books. It seems empty. Looking around, I touch a book, then pull it from the shelves.

Earthly ventures consume you. . . so off track. Turn the page to see truth.

Oh, a flowing light soul. It is mine, free of daily concerns—growing, pulsing, connected to one and all things.

I touch the book and feel the connection to myself. My fingers on my soul—unwounded, uncluttered, my true nature of light, divine.

Wouldn't it be nice if you could live that instead of the earthly choices distracting you today?

Your despair is linked to fear. Those voices are showers of protection, but so much blockage from truth, the ego, the divine. Two forces at battle within you. Perhaps it should not be seen as a battle because that stance serves to put you on the defensive as if finding the divine and letting it flourish could hurt you.

Why is the trail to the divine such a threat? Who benefits from that?

No one but the rabble of human injury speaks, anyway. Why devote power there?

Choice. You know, of course, the power of that and yet sometimes it feels like you have none or you are vastly overwhelmed by that responsibility. Too much. No one to blame but self for your unhappiness.

All a muddle. If this resides in you, which it does, why the focus on ego? Does this make you weak? Faulty? Marred by flaws you cannot control? Or merely human?

At root seems to be acceptance and choice. Perhaps if you ponder relationship between those two factors you will get some enlightenment. Your failure to manage the voices causes despair, which triggers shame because you know you have a choice and are making the wrong one.

We keep bringing up shame as motivator. If pure soul of light, what is source of shame? How is it controlling you? How is it tied to all other feelings of failure? Worth? Anger?

I see two forces in you and you have the choice between page of darkness and page of light. Now, how not to blame self and feel shame for letting darkness creep in two pages facing self/each other. Glowing light of divine connection. Darkness of earthly concerns. Ego. Fears. Despair. Yet choice seems simple—shame on you.

Are you looking to us for answers to that eternal question to escape the idea of choice?

Is it really a choice? Perhaps it is something else.

It is. It just is. They are both there. They reside in you. They are you, they just are. Is it really an either/or? Is it just IS? Can you accept that it just is?

Yes, there is shame. Fear triggers insecurity while human. Fact of life and yet your glowing soul resides in you, too. Not really separate, just hidden, ignored, underappreciated. Perhaps the two should not be facing one another on separate pages. Do they belong on same page so that you can try to accept both to reside side by side? Could the two hold hands? Can they coexist?

Wait, they already do! It is you that separates into good, bad, darkness and light. Yes, they are not separate choices, not constant pressure to choose and failure when you don't. Can we eliminate the fold of the book and put it all on the same plane and just realize they both are and one gets more attention, but it doesn't have to? It may just be louder because it is more dominant while on earth, but don't forget you don't lose otherworldly. You just spend less time on it. Not enough attention paid. No tribute given. See if in mind's eye you can envision entire tableau of self and self in universe, instead of just self as flawed wife, mother, person, worrying about creating safe spaces and safe relationships. Creating boxes just prevents you from seeing vista, but do not see this as choice. It is merely attention paid. You forget to look, envision, nurture as it is not part of the trip to the store, but can it be more of you in the everyday? Can you try to find a way to see it as just making sure to visit, attend to, develop, rather than feel bad for not making constant choices to see good?

You have much of the time seen life in terms of good/bad and carried weight of choices with you. Every day you 'choose' to see darkness weighs heavily. The guilt you feel and the shame you feel by making bad choices further blocks the view.

How about a lot less judgment and a lot more nurturing of all sides of you?

Acknowledge. They. Are. Say hey, draw that vista. See if talking to light self can help instead of just choosing to try to talk dark voices down off the ledge. Hey, I see light, too. They are both me—one deprived of recognition and power and one taking on more than it deserves. Shame about choice and guilt needs a healthier place to live. Release that light. You can see it and feel it. It has its power, too!

How about you make peace with both aspects of self? Heal that rift. End that war. Give yourself a break!

Truce is healing. To be happier you must heal by bringing harmony to both sides.

That is a lot to process. Take your time. Sit here. Look at that light. Envision the vista in you that better reflects the universe that surrounds you.

It is heat. It is light and darkness. Cold. Collision. Symbiosis. Power of life. Good and bad. These things just are. As are you.

Steps
Reading 11

The connections will come from your steps, not your plans.

You have been hearing us all morning. We have been bugging you—listen to us! You can feel the life shift occurring, but you have only been mulling it. Now it is time to get down to business and see where that takes us.

I would like to know where this is going.

Well, wouldn't we all? It is going, that is all you need to know. This journey will require you to stop anticipating the path and all its choices and diversions as a far-off possibility. You have lived life as a planner. You want to know what point a, b and c will bring and how to arrive at d, which is the best possible outcome.

That must stop. Now. Please envision the path as a journey you take into a field, one step at a time, and the only thing that appears is the next touchstone. One at a time. There is no touchstone two. Get comfortable with just enjoying this reading as one step. See the path before you? Nope. No path. Just endless possibility. Who knows where this will take you?

I see before me a brilliant, green pasture and a horizon. The pasture is untouched by human footprints. It is virgin pasture. Trees line the vast expanse of green and the blue horizon is beautiful, but it is completely open. There are no barriers, impediments, clouds, paths or distractions. It is my new journey in front of me—unfettered, open, beautifully undecided—just open possibility.

Can you keep that vision in your mind as you proceed? You will need it when you get discouraged or wonder about direction or wonder about outcomes. The steps forward are the outcome. Do you see there is no destination in front of you, just horizon and possibility? We gave you this as an earthly metaphor, but you do know it streams into the universe you envision in your visits. It, too, is vast with no determined direction.

Why isn't the vision (of the pasture) showing connection when the universe teems with connection?

The connections will come from your steps, not your plans. Although you see this as disconnected, you are mistaken. There are people who will connect with you in this journey. You haven't met them yet and they are irrelevant. It is your journey. If you can transpose the two images, pasture and universe, you will be able to see those are reflective of one another, though disparate in nature. Linking two will be interesting activity for your development.

We can sense your joy at coming home. We hope you can feel our joy at you making this decision to put next foot forward into the pasture. Just next step.

Ponder that next step, but don't worry unduly about its direction. Steps can always be taken again and differently or in a new way. No path is set in stone, so do not worry about next step too much.

You seem to have come up with a step forward into pasture, one designed to provide you with what you need to nurture this step.

Gather information that allows you to understand your gifts.

Try to find a few people to help you in the journey. You only need a few. Find someone or something in step with you—novice beginning journey, willing to discover. Not sure where that will come from yet, but good idea.

History becomes history with each step forward. It doesn't become determined in the future. It is always defined in the past. Ponder that. Today's step becomes tomorrow's history, but it does not become predetermined future at all. Are you getting my point? Path determined as a path in retrospect, not in anticipation. A big concept for you to ponder!

Pasture image is for the human. Universe image is truly spirit vision. Residing in both worlds requires understanding of that difference. History itself is a human construct.

For now, that seems like plenty for a first step. Look down on your feet in those ruby slippers as they take you forward one beautiful, hopeful step at a time.

Swirl
Reading 12

You must own a box full of mysteries as proudly as you exhibit your box full of expansions.

Here is the tape. Why? How? Who? When? How do I fix this? Why am I like that? How does my past influence that? What is in my future?

In your review of this awakening, the swirling concerns keep, well, swirling. Same concerns over and over and over and over.

Swirl. Swirl. Swirl. Get the metaphor of the swirl?

You need to recognize these repetitive concerns as just that; they reside in a swirl round and round and round they go.

UNANSWERABLE!

You even keep asking why about that!

Okay. Let's start anew. As a spiritual being in a human body your quest is to expand authentic self on soul's journey. Seek answers—and acceptance key.

Here is what you are missing, what you are ignoring. So far, you refuse to accept the reality that there are just some things about yourself that you cannot know—now and here—or ever.

That does not negate the quest. It merely expands it once again in graceful acceptance; shift constraint, focus circular 'why, oh why' to acceptance that the answer does not exist now.

Maybe it is just beyond your incarnation here. The veil is heavy between what we know in body and what we understand in spirit. There is a reason for that—learning through struggle.

If you could always just look to the back of the book for answers, what would you learn? What if all tests came with the answers? In both cases, would there be an impetus to learn? Struggle with the reality of complex existence?

No.

You would all be peeking at the answers, complacent with the fact you knew something for the moment but are now set.

Growth comes through struggle, limitation, challenge, endurance—not from complacency or peeking—the easy way.

Spiritual development is very challenging. It requires wrestling with the things we know, the things we learn and the things we can never grasp because we are never designed to grasp them. There are some things we cannot grasp.

Put these in their proper place in your journey. They are not worthy of your struggle. They are a mystery, not designed for human consumption. Expand questions to include that bin—the swirl questions not intended for current growth.

No, we cannot tell you what those questions are, for they are entirely unique to each authentic soul's development. Then how will you know what to put in that bin? Your unanswerable?

Look at a recurring quest in your journey. Examine it. For example, "Why I have always been so _____?" If this has been a lifelong struggle for you clearly as a pattern, it may reside on a soul level with no human experiences to address it. Perhaps it is not for you to completely understand while here. If any question seems to arise out of past human origins, but all subsequent life choices have failed to alleviate it and still leaves you in that swirling question, perhaps it isn't for you here.

At some point you must be able to say you can continue your journey without knowing that. Don't allow it to continue consuming your energy. Just yes, it is there. The insight may come later through experience. That answer may never come. Possibly, there is no answer.

Continuing the journey is all about rejoicing in the discoveries and expansion your daily choices bring to you. Ceding power to unanswered mysteries does nothing to further that end.

As you review your review of your review, give name to the holes you allow to have sway over you. Some things just aren't for you to know. Simple as that.

Seeing, acknowledging, accepting and releasing transfers the power of the unknown in your hands. You must own a box full of mysteries as proudly as you exhibit your box full of expansions.

All in flux. All as is. Better yet, no boxes. All in same heart. Moving along. Dancing in place.

Ironically, your mind is racing to write the ending of this. Did you just not learn anything about the swirl?

You keep asking, how does this make sense? Fit in? You want closure when there is none. Ending while open is best.

Leave it open and unknown—the first of your mysteries to accept.

Acceptance
Reading 13

Heal rifts rending self.

Plea to self / world

Self really key—how divisive are the conflicts that reside in you?
If you don't accept yourself, how will the rest of the world be able to?
United front of self—all voices integrate into peaceful, united entity.
End the competition to be heard—heal rifts rending self.
Not a competition; rather comfort.

Humanity must nurture all three—mind, spirit and heart—for development.
Balance:
Too much spirit=fanaticism
Too much mind= detached intellectualism
Too much heart= Inability to see truth

Now
Reading 14

Live only here.

Now is a gentle pause between
past and future.

What was, is and shall be
All tightly entwined

Some peace-
some not so much

Live only here

As twins
Exist merely as remnants
. . . Or possibilities

Today has the lights on
Teeming with life whooshing by

Don't forget to look!

Time
Reading 15

The tick tock you think, matters, naught.

No hurry-

What time? Does it matter?

To fill days with lists of soul-
less activity

More the heartbeat

Drums that echo with longing
To hear you pulse with life
Listen to the call

The tick tock
You think matters

Naught

Life is too short, but is it? By what definition? Time merely exists—it is.

You are here, then you aren't. You have just so much of it.

Time—words/concepts associated with it. Not enough, tight, rushing, too much time on your hands, not enough to do. Some judgments—wasting time, using it wisely, good choices. Making poor time choices modern crime against humanity. Are you wasting it? Making the most of every minute? Being a good steward of the time allotment you have been given?

Your obituary is a paean to your use of time: dedicated, loving, devoted, hard-working, family-oriented, sacrificing— spin that tries to convince you made the best use of the time you had been given. You had fun, worked hard, spread joy. You accomplished much; you made a difference in lives. Loved ones surrounded you at the end because of your efforts.

And yet—

What does all that mean? Define the life: money made, activities, hobbies, devotion to others. A life's list describing how you used your time.

But here is just a short spark among infinite others. "Making the most of it" a human construct to help explain why you are here.

It would appear at first glance some are more here than others, which is an impossible yardstick.

And yet we are all here for the same reason. To live out a cycle of energy in a human body with all life's frailty and hopefully develop as souls, deepen our energy connection to all universal energy. No one chalks up any more points than any other—the flow continues. Different plane, different measurement.

Ponder human construct of time and what it means and what it does not.

PS- Install an on/off switch.

Answers

Reading 16

Today's cautionary topic—answers. There are none.

So, you think you have it now
Clenched in fist

Such hubris!
Quicksilver leaks, dripping, drip, drop
Escaping grasp

Lesson here:
Certainty not a thing—
        Never has been
        Never will be

Life in flashes—
Who can own a blink of an eye called insight?
Come on, now
Let it go

Be happy with brilliant sparkles
Rather than heavy tomes.

• • • • • • • • •

Today's cautionary topic—answers. There are none. Or if they come, their purpose only serves the moment and nothing more.

Think of humans walking around with blinders—and goggles. All the eyeglasses in the world can't cure that myopic view of the world.

We are purposefully given limited sight to foster struggle, which fosters learning.

Some people have/are given/develop/come with sight that is a bit clearer. But even that is limited in its scope because humanity wounds us and because it is our foot in the hole (or that caused the hole), we can't see it unfold in its entirety.

Our foot hurts. We are in danger. We carelessly caused the accident by our inherently limited vision. So, to live and see clearly is to vow to keep looking, not for the answer, but for the little piece of sky blue needed to complete the corner of the puzzle.

Accept this: Your goal is not to die with a finished puzzle. It shape-shifts throughout life and you are only working to somewhat comprehend a small piece of its enigma.

In looking for the small slivers of blue, you are just looking to connect it to something larger and appreciate its unique features and perhaps appreciate its beauty in its entirety.

Perhaps peace really does lie in the appreciation of the vision that allows you the lens to find the elusive, beautiful piece lying hidden among all others.

There is great satisfaction in small things—pieces, daily rituals, flowers, cups of coffee, insights. Release the frustration of trying to envision or complete the whole landscape before you. Pieces can be beautiful and hold power, too.

Today the puzzle piece is perhaps irregular in shape, blue with a tiny speck of a sun's ray in the corner. Where does it fit? Does it need to fit, or is it good enough for its brilliant blue and flash of yellow? If it finds its place in the whole, that is great! If not, it remains beautiful nonetheless. Is life about completing the puzzle or loving the blue?

Perhaps it is all those things with due appreciation for all steps; seeing the piece, loving the spark of yellow and trying to find its rightful home in the universe—all equally good.

No need to finish it this time around. Oops! There is no finish.

Even sandcastles have their time to shine, wash away and return in some other incarnation—or just sparkle as grains of sand.

Paradox

Reading 17

Barriers are constructed here to cover the holes in the heart.

Reside in this space
Moment, time, flash
Among all others in entirety
Endless in scope—beginning of time
End of it, too

Who shall see it all?

Not I, who was given a most narrow lens
As were you

Peering, struggling to see beyond
The boundaries of the pinprick given to us
Merely that . . . and nothing (so much) more

• • • • • • • • • •

Brilliant morning,

Barriers of all sorts are the plague of mankind.

We experience many: between local hearts, souls united,
countries, citizens, earth and universe. Everything exists in
micro and macro.

Life is more snow globe than scenic pasture. Settle—shift—
settle—shift. Those that seek to reside in the land of settled
are missing all the excitement of the whirl.

What if in shaking the globe you expose the beauty of the question and the excitement of the change? There is nothing to fear from flying about. You may even land somewhere better.

A chance exists that the globe will shatter and you may feel the expanse of a wider world far beyond the confines of where you currently hide.

Some have pretended to venture beyond by convincing themselves there is one path out and adhering to that belief that they and like-minded beings will weather the storm and head to heavenly sanctuary unscathed and valued above all others.

Wrong.

It is a crowded place beyond and all are welcome to congregate in unity of connection.

Such a paradox. Barriers here. Connection there. Existing so closely side by side, parted only by a thin veil. Peek under the veil to embrace energy of the beyond. Don't wear the blinders here of assured path to an exclusionary nirvana.

You will be surprised by the vastness stretching before you— and your own willingness to embrace all beings with strands of connection to you. Lovely to feel that here instead of waiting. But barriers are constructed here to cover the holes in the heart. Our cosmic duty is to heal those wounds and become a stronger soul.

We are all in it together, here and there.

Truly.

Watch the flowers reach for the sun. You, too!

Journey
Reading 18

Refrain from postponing life until you get 'there'. There is no 'there'.

Greetings on such a lovely, sunny day of enlightenment!

You keep trying to peer into the future of this. In doing so, you lessen the potential energy by saying now is not as important as arriving at destination. When taking a trip, destination seems like only goal, but isn't the travel to and from equally enlightening? You can't enjoy the trip until you get there? Nonsense!

So, what is this trip you are on? People waving as you pass by. Lessons to be learned. Development of the self—of soul: patience, empathy, insight, connection, soul development.

Soul travel! Look out the window to see, notice and appreciate all that journey entails. Another interesting paradox; all above imply you are passing through and yet learning/seeing much. Just observer, untouched by the weather.

Perhaps a slow stroll would be a better metaphor. That way you are immersed in it. Feel the energy, note the connections. So what if your 'journey' takes so much longer? Longer than what? Journey implies you are heading someplace particular.

Remember there are no answers? Think about the fact there may actually be no destination. Well, that is not entirely accurate.

Death is the only destination for all human forms. For spirit, death is not a destination; it is a rest stop.

So, when you fret about where this is going, you are ignoring the fact of death, but also the transient nature of spirit development—applying limited human vision to reality of what an infinite journey really is.

As you begin your leg of the journey today, walk about with an awareness of moment in time and refrain from postponing life until you get *there*. There is no *there*.

There is only here—and here can be glorious in resplendent beauty and that value is not diminished by being merely a step forward to a nonexistent, imaginary better place/destination.

Today you are at your destination. You have arrived. Gather your belongings and exit the cabin. You are here.

Discernment
Reading 19

Tickling out the light and dark IS the soul growth opportunity.

Greetings on this lovely day of gray.

Light, dark, gray—not just colors of the weather, also colors in spirit spectrum.

Light—that which you know and are given to enlighten, illuminate, connect, refresh, stimulate growth.

Dark—that which you hide. It is your self-imposed inability to see, cloak of protection, denial of truth, oppression, suppression, retreat, agent of isolation, emotional bunker of false security.

Which leads us to today's gray—where most of human experiences reside.

Periods of light promote growth, periods of dark arrest development—so for the most part we reside in gray. Like an artist's brush, we swirl together light and dark to make it so.

Why? Because both alternatives are hard to take.

Light can be puzzling, overwhelming and misleading above all else. To us it is not to be trusted. The world does not embrace light full on; so much hostility, so much disregard for truth, so much bending of life to fit personal narratives. Even so, light can masquerade in Halloween attire.

The 'light' of an exclusionary worship is a personal narrative rather than universal truth. It simplifies uncertainty of human progress. It negates difficult contemplation by purchasing an insurance policy that makes life easier here and falsely guarantees a lovely afterlife with little effort or investment which is a fool's path.

Darkness can masquerade as light in the form of hate and prejudice that lifts your spirits and gives clear purpose to your life.

Gray is so much harder to grasp.

The swirling of light and dark each day IS the struggle for growth. What is right? What is true? How to live honorably, without using light or dark to ease the unease of humanity?

Embrace it. Tickling out the light and dark IS the soul growth opportunity in the shifting, everyday of man. Work, it takes work, and thought, and the utmost self-awareness.

A very frightful place for many humans. But, it is not meant to say one person cannot worry about all human choices. You must only worry about your own and speak your own as they are unveiled to you. If it is truth, its ripples will wash over others in the intersection of souls and the impact may be felt—or not—based on the other soul's desire to see.

Whether it does or not is not relevant here. Attend to your own soul growth. Tease the light from the dark and see both. Relish the light in all its glory and allow your soul to expand under its careful guidance. Be wary of the dark as it casts shade and stunts development.

Gray days abound and soul growth depends on them for challenge.

Listen to the voice within for guidance. Learn to discern between it and the voices you have acquired due to your life experiences—the frightened five-year-old, the wounded wife.

Discernment is key to soul growth. Shut down the noise. Listen to the voices light and dark. See as clearly as being human allows you to. The window may be small and the day gray, but truth exists in each and every moment you choose to listen.

Open eyes. Open ears. Open heart. Open mind.

Open soul is yours for the asking.

Self

Reading 20

Harness the oneness of here and there for strength in journey.

Good morning. Oh, where to begin?

First, continue on your path to self-discovery and universal revelation. Search is one and the same. You are just beginning to see a glimpse of a tiny fraction of a pinprick—enlightened you are not—but the journey entails widening the pinprick to see a bigger piece of a grand universe of connection that is fairly incomprehensible to human spirits-in-training.

But if you stay with it you will have fun and grow spiritually in ways currently unimaginable for you.

Envision stardust being tossed over you in all its delight. Do not let fear darken the door. We can feel it haunt you. *You are alone in this. Who understands? You need others to make your way. . .* or do you?

Alone is you. It has always been such. Not saying finding a tribe isn't comforting—just unnecessary at this time. You are exploring your soul in its present form.

Resist the pull of outside definition and interference. Some information is necessary but stick to guidance that is procedural rather than experiential. Your experience is not anyone else's, thus resist the desire to replicate it.

Learn what is going on in you. Try some suggestions that might aid in your journey. Reach out to others for some interaction, but until you have clarified parameters of your own experience, do not seek answers for or from others.

Deal with alone vs. lonely. You are not alone in this at all—

Focus on trying to connect to those with souls outreached in your direction. Be careful of any lines you draw.

In many respects, this is you again on the slushy ice with one foot away from disaster. But remember, your soul has expanded through your experiences. All those voices from the past want most of all to protect you.

Harness the oneness of here and there for strength in journey.

We understand the problem with earthly family and bemoan it. It will hinder you but be gentle with yourself in it. Your view of things may expand enough to see that open hand offering hope. If not, you can discuss it when you pass. Your life here together was no accident.

In short, continue. Can you hear them clapping? Many here are happy for you and will help in any way. Learn to ask. It is a resource you are missing and will help if you can tap into it.

· · · · · · · · ·

Searching

See the intrepid spider
That ventured into vast,
white expanse.

Alone.

Wildly in search of what he needs
Not sure it is out there

But-
does it anyway

Why Not?

What good is safety in a dark corner
when you can live free?

Unity
Reading 21

Caution must be taken to avoid balms that ease pain,
but do not heal wounds.

Psychology—what you function with while in human form;
temperament, experiences, intellect, emotions, family . . .
unique manifestation of earthly you. The complex mix of
you as a human and how it affects how you live out your life
in thoughts, choices, actions.

Spiritual being, soul self, your eternal self resides in you but is
relegated to background for the most part, unless brought out
of the shadows and placed in the spotlight to bask in the glow
of acceptance and expand in the security of understanding.

Spirit is an integral part to a healthy psychology and provides
something/a view/insight/bigger than merely human eyes. It
can help us heal the wounds and fill the holes that impede
our growth in unhealthy ways, if it is practiced authentically.

Caution must be taken to avoid balms that ease pain, but do
not heal wounds. Alcohol, drugs, devotions that do not
embrace a universal spirit are self-deceptive behaviors that
blot out the truth. I feel better, but I am not healthy because
I have not healed damaging wounds.

To have a healthy self all must be accepted and embraced;
your temperament, experiences, choices, emotions, time and
place, relationships to others and most importantly, spirit are
all working in tandem towards self-actualization if you are
courageous to work toward unity, acceptance and peace.

It awaits all those who peer within and accept the 'without'—unconditionally and with <u>love</u>.

You have always known it comes to this, but you always believed it entailed your ability to love others and thought you had to be good enough for people to love you. You thought it only came to the deserving.

It only comes to the accepting:
1) Love your authentic self first;
2) Look with loving eyes on others;
3) Approach the world with a loving heart.

Whether someone loves you or not has nothing to do with you as a loving spirit. It is wonderful if they do, but until you love yourself, deep wounds within you cannot heal; deep holes within you cannot be filled with the love of others. They are filled by loving your true spirit self and developing a courageous love and acceptance of others and the world.

Let this wash over you in waves of revelation.

True earthly satisfaction lies in uniting the complex psychology with the glue of eternal self as it pertains to an earthly life—center it around love and work from there.

Healing our holes and wounds can lead us to happy places.

Love is possible because you can/must love your soul-self first. Start there. That takes away the wait for others to love you because you deserve it. You can love self openly, without conditions because eternal soul self is loving entity. It is love, purely so.

Love others as best you can. In all cases, expect and accept imperfection. Love is the greatest challenge as humans tangle with psychology and spirit—human emotion and experiences limit, while loving spirit can expand our vast capacity to embrace growth beyond that which we experience here. Such a hard concept to grasp through this little peephole!

Music
Reading 22

You will have to decide if to dance, when to dance and how to dance.

Today is an interesting day. You have been told there are plans so stay tuned—and yet, what to do until plans become clearer? Very human question of you.

Treasures are in every day and your daily plan should be to uncover them as they unfold. Even if spiritual masters have discussed using you, the 'plan' for humans consists of living daily in a state of wonder and joy in breathing.

You cannot peer into the future for details of any plan. You aren't the planner—you are the implementer, the instrument of something bigger. You truly cannot make the plan. You can listen for the strains of the music and dance to them. What a joyous activity for you!

Of course, there will be choices for you along the way, but we repeat, you are not the composer of this masterpiece or the architect of this construction. You are the dancer, so you will have to decide if to dance, when to dance and how to dance...but the dance goes on without you.

When you choose to dance, you get included in the activities. When you choose not to dance or be open to new music, the music/song/dance continues without you, but you are merely sidelined.

So, pick up your feet and be open to the music. You will hear its strains increasingly louder in the future if you open your mind and heart to its infinite beauty.

When you viewed the universe before, you did not hear a sound. Now add music to your vision for a deeper understanding of the complexity in the universe.

As a human, you can participate in your own spiritual development, not by fumbling, but through joyful choice about how to expand your view of this matrix and your role in it. You have indeed chosen and your offer has been accepted.

Be aware of your wildest dreams for even as your life plays out in its human parameters, the possibility for spiritual expansion is great—if you choose . . . daily . . . to dance.

Co-creation
Reading 23

Opportunity cannot cross your path unless you create one.

Relax and open the mind's eye.

So, your worldly distress threatens to overwhelm you. In questions. In doubt. In despair.

Welcome to humanity.

Now, however, you lack the human shield of activity to divert your attention. You seem to lack balance. You have experienced information overload. You are taking in the world.

The aloneness you feel is lack of alleviation of that. You long for more because you want to escape and you feel trapped, without escape.

And yet you have it?

You are experimenting with the power of control. In a world with wide open flow, both here and there, with energy flowing from here, you are inundated with <u>too much!</u>

Battle of negative world energy and light of positive soul energy. Your reaction is worldly—dismay and floundering. Take a moment to assess priority. We contend it is time to temper absorption with engagement. Action will temper overflow of worldly dismay.

Think of one, two or more actions you can take daily to replace habit—yes, habit—of earthly information inundation.

Choose action: create something, bake bread, arrange interactions, experience new realms, paint, cook, read fiction—do!

For now, accept aloneness as part of this venture. We do not believe future holds that for you, but you cannot connect unless you forget the path. You have been waiting for <u>THE THING</u> to cross your path, and yet you did nothing to form the path . . . or when you did, it wasn't the right path for you. You have to revise your view of opportunity.

By living and walking the right path, you are <u>co-creator.</u> Life is not given. Opportunity is not given. Life is <u>created</u> through action. The path forward is created daily through endeavors. Magical thinking to believe if you sit by the window, life will knock on your door.

What is your responsibility in creating the path? These are your feet doing the walking. Opportunity cannot cross your path unless you create one. It would behoove you to look at the near past or perhaps your entire life through the lens of paths—chosen or otherwise.

Seemingly otherwise. Because it is always a choice (the next step to take), there should be no worries about the right step or the wrong step. There are only steps of equal measure; right and wrong is only a human construct assessment through a rear-view mirror.

Next step—pause button on absorption. Pause button on engagement. Next step on path is to sit a spell. Assess. Reflect. Plot out past path in terms of life creation.

Look at those voices inside and on paper—meet them. Understand the steps you took. The paths you created and why. Hear them as they narrate your life. See life with new eyes and an open, unjudgmental heart.

Remember—this is not a struggle—or a time of painful re-creation of failed opportunities. It is a continuing chapter in the unfolding story of your growth and self-awareness.

Next time you will work on the puzzle of your life—unfinished always. But such work will lead to sense, awareness and healing, with the intention of making each daily step more meaningful, bathed in awareness.

Thus, when you engage on the path again, activity will not be a shield or a balm. It will be nurturing, a flourishing soul as it develops its true self. Your steps there can be an explosion of color in soul energy—and a subtle healing in your infinite soul's plan.

Such a gift before you leave earth this time and bring with you new insight.

Human wounds healed facilitate soul growth. Let these healing waves wash over you. Swim in the universal ocean—warm, safe, open.

Then dry off and get back on the path with enhanced understanding and spiritual power.

What more?

Isn't that enough?

Change
Reading 24

We are just shells in the ocean churning around in its turbulent waves.

Interesting dichotomy with modern life.

We are in a time of tremendous shifting under our feet and yet our lives seem to only be changing in small, disquieting ways.

We look around us and see our lives changing incrementally—yet—we look down at our feet and know the very bedrock of the earth's crust (and human life) is shifting due to forces we cannot see. All we feel is the vague rumblings and it makes us afraid, uncertain, disquieted.

The certainties we counted on are failing us: jobs, education, government, families. In all these areas, technology is the catalyst in vast ways we do not understand and cannot begin to control, rendering us seemingly powerless.

All require comprehensive view we are incapable of seeing, managing, handling as humans.

We are just shells in the ocean churning around in its turbulent waves, washing on the shore changed by the pressure of forces we cannot begin to influence.

In our small, fearful hearts we are gasping for air, floundering in a sea much bigger than ourselves—soulfully choking while watching the sea change. 'Please, just settle down' we cry. We want the earth beneath our feet and our small, fearful hearts to stop quaking. We want to stop quaking! But that will not happen.

This is part of what has always been, only some periods and events are more impactful than others. The earth quivers, or rumbles. It shakes and sometimes it cracks—sometimes even explodes—and sometimes it rests. Now is a time of great shifting and cracking and for some, explosions large and small.

We are grabbing for something/someone/anything to stabilize us. All we can do is stabilize ourselves and hang on. Buckle up for the ride—and recognize what is going on in this time and this place—and accept it for what it is.

Put this out into the universe somehow. That is all.

These are not mere ramblings. You are being given these for a reason. We can only give them to you. You have to be the translator, the intermediary.

Ponder what to do. No need for money. No need for fame. Just convey the message. The forces causing this also provide possibility/opportunity.

Ponder that.

Clarity

Reading 25

It is a magical journey to see,
understand and embrace spirit with human eyes.

Good morning,
You have much to do today.

Life examination in eyes growing larger, vision improving,
clarity into self. Awareness of self key to soul growth. It is
self-awareness, self-knowledge. Soul knowledge.

So few endeavor to undertake it, for as you know, it is filled
with human suffering that is your own and it requires the
objectivity and empathy to seek your own answers.

Few humans undertake the quest, so soul growth tends to be
slow over the eons of endeavors. The window of insight is
small. On occasion, the window widens and some humans
get a rare opportunity to reside between the internal and the
external—and see both—and see how they are intertwined
and really are not two but are one. The walls between in and
out, here and there, soul and ego can be thick and dark—
sometimes fading to opaque, translucent, transparent and
finally gone entirely.

In reality, you are at translucent/transparent. There is light
and sometimes it is clear, but the wall remains.

This life review brings you to greater understanding of wall
construction, but it remains to be seen how much you will
transcend to see. It is your vision. You are the leader here.
Courageous undertaking can lead to self-knowledge which

can lead to enlightenment and maybe greater clarity and understanding of universal matrix.

Or not.

It is a magical journey to see, understand and embrace spirit with human eyes—a gift you have planned with spirit to grow in grace.

The vision you have experienced floating in universal energy is not merely something you have seen. It is really where your spirit resides and you have seen it while human, which allows you as self to expand in your growth toward universal submersion.

Ah yes, you know you are one with God and one with each other with unique soul identities and connections to the divine. Your faulty earthly eyes hinder this comprehension, but humans are not destined to live divinely, so it is not detrimental.

Humanity is our challenge, our opportunity to grow beyond that which binds us and blinds us here—take advantage of that struggle. Embrace the pain as the fire that shapes us into more empathetic spirits.

The hot light of pain feeds the fire that consumes the Phoenix—to rise again—and again—and again—the same, yet reborn better in spirit. Able to help others with journey to expanded spirit.

Paradoxes again: human/spirit, pain/joy, pinprick focus/spiritual expansion, turmoil/healing, limited vision/soul clarity.

Feel the small, pained human in you and how she was periodically entwined with a quest to know more about the beckoning light of spirit. Go to her today. One more time. This time. In a journey that repeats itself, that will repeat itself here and over eons.

Your journey is all journeys. Embrace it moving toward light.

Give thanks for gifts you are about to receive. Treasures, one and all.

Healing

Reading 26

This is toil that is not for the faint of heart, but rather for the strong in heart spirit.

We are all looking for something. Actually, we are all looking for the same thing—love (=acceptance=peace w/self=safety=belonging).

When feeling disconnected, unsafe, we go into protective crouch. Being out of place makes us feel bewildered. Who are we? Who loves and accepts us? Who feeds our soul in connection, safety, acceptance?

In truth, we must do that for self and build connection from there—rather than reverse. We must build that from inside, rather than outside in. Much harder! Requires healing, introspection, self-healing. Depression, paralysis, 'laziness', inactivity, isolation all result from this cutting of external ties and resulting detachment. Yet those external ties are so transient!

We have to build own ties to loving self and move on from there. Must heal self. No external situation can do that for you, and until that is done, people live life on broken, slushy ice—afraid to move, looking for easy way to land, a helping hand to steady and save. BUT you are the only helping hand that matters, the only one who can steady the ice and live joyously.

It is good to have external connections (friends, jobs), but they cannot heal the wounds or fill the holes. They serve as great balm and convince you that all is well, you are fine until the ice shifts and the hole is revealed and uncertainty reigns again.

But external is always transitory. All come and go. Best gift you can give yourself is yourself—whole and accepted by self as self. Self-love is recognition of the true divine that is your piece of the universal connection to a higher power.

We come here to learn from human-inflicted holes and wounds. We do it again and again until we remove the human-view mirror and install a window instead and reside in the place that accepts you and your place in the universe, flaws and all. And you can love yourself in spite of them.

The love of others is wonderful, but it is not a substitute for loving and accepting yourself. First healing, so that love can flow from you outward, reversing the course to a healthier, healing flow.

Scars, open wounds and holes are caused by what you needed and didn't get. All reside in you waiting to provide insight, growth and self-acceptance. This is toil that is not for the faint of heart, but rather for the strong in heart spirit. This struggle will never end as long as you remain in human form, but the potential for grace and soul expansion is great, for those who venture into this pain and darkness.

Human, venture to heal thyself.

Love
Reading 27

Know there is hope—and love—for you.

Good morning! Welcome back!

It has been awhile and we have patiently watched as you struggled with the most earthly lesson of all—love. And you have been engulfed by the great pain its absence wrecks upon the human spirit.

You have always suspected love was key, but because you didn't know of it or experience it in your early life, you had created a great struggle for yourself to ponder.

Love is the key, so take love away and what do you have? Isolation. Pain. A life disconnected from the vitality of others' beating hearts.

You lived alone, without love to see how it felt, its impact on the spirit.

And now that you see the love/not love comparison, you are ready to heal and move forth into love for the remainder of your life. Your darkness was the blackened hole created by lack of love. It was your deepest fears come to life. Alone. Dark. Unworthy. Disconnected.

You had tried to create love in that home through your gift of children. For them you learned to love in spite of its dangers. Leaving that place frightened you. Was that the end of it? Did you return to that unloved place as an unloved child who was invisible and in life alone?

On the other side of the tunnel, the warmth of love beckons to you ever stronger. You came out battered, but your inner resilience has proved elastic once again and instead of a heart cloaked in darkness, you see a heart that is deserving of light.

The scars you carry with you can heal. The holes in your spirit can be filled.

You know that is why we come here—to use earthly, mortal experiences to learn larger spiritual lessons.

You have undertaken this task from the beginning. Despite the dark circumstances of your past, your strength of spirit, your resilience always endures. Although darkness threatened to crush your spirit, it never did. You always used your insatiable quest to know, to seek answers. Even in your darkest hour you knew to seek hope through questions, knowledge, clarity, knowing—always fighting for a better way even when there seemed to be no way.

Continue your journey of human/spiritual discovery. Many answers still await you. Accept the now for what it is—pain, healing, hope. Also accept this is the path of your life, a chosen path. Understand your dynamic as the path this time through and you will accept the inevitable ebb and flow that is inherent in your struggle. Know there will be struggle. Know there is deeply embedded resilience.

Know there is hope—and love—for you.

You may have been denied an earthly love, but you were never without divine love. You may have felt earthly alone, but you always had deep connection to the universal spirit. Both of those proved to be a light to lead you out of darkness in the painful earthly journey you have chosen. Love and connection have always been yours here; now your spirit becomes awakened to them there.

Enlightenment is a gift of the spirit, by the spirit, to the spirit. You have chosen to participate in a difficult journey.

Godspeed.

Whole

Whole—unite earthly and spiritual using eyes flawed somewhat by both.

How appropriate! You wrote first page upside down, out of sync. Nothing is accidental.

Now you can visualize your human existence. The words are right there next to these, but you cannot read them due to your physical limitations. And yet, we said them clearly, we stated spiritual truths and now you cannot easily access them because your eyes won't allow it unless you expend effort to flip this and see things clearly.

Flipping back and forth—being human.

But we are on same page, yes? We can see it there, but limits make it hard to see.

Here and there merely a physical construct, not a spiritual one.

There is no here and there.

There is just—IS, the verb to be.

Such an artificial division fostered by the presence of a body, influenced by experiences in the body.

Human life batters the spirit in its weakness. We go into body and we become vulnerable, uncertain. We are self but take on impediments necessary to foster growth.

Here and there—not really.

Same. Must accept what you are in spirit is always; what you are as human challenges how you see it. Both are you nonetheless. One being. Here and there at same time, both are just one.

So, your struggle with human form is spirit working to expand self to better awareness—to improve vision to be all encompassing. To grow and help others grow.

If energy is the connection to the divine and you are pulsing energy striving to become purer light, then your journey connects to all journeys to unite with the divine energy. Interconnected all—some seeing, some not.

Expand your understanding to see how life examination there is spirit examination here. All same examination for expansion of energy in divine image.

So, as you grapple with human pain, connect to soul expansion. No such boundary exists unless you construct it in limited thinking. When you are looking at you as human being, see your experiences in terms of spiritual development. You must see whole self. It is up to you. That is why we are telling you this.

The line you are seeing does not really exist! You are/can be free of it. Seeing earthly pain as spiritual struggle in divine light will open you to growth unlimited, healing soul self, whole self. Whole—unite earthly and spiritual using eyes flawed somewhat by both.

No, not conjoined twins.

Self as it exists in different forms in different times, blinded by different limits every time. Spiritual awakening involves seeing two as one and tearing down the artificial construct between here and there.

You ARE one.

The puzzle of one includes humanity and spirit together.
Now try to eliminate words: together, both, here/there.
Expand mind to encompass one. Feel divine embrace of you
whole in all incarnations.

I am spirit—sometimes spirit in body and sometimes spirit out of body.
I am spirit.
I am spirit connected to divine spirit. I am spark of the divine that
exists in all life.

Right now, you are writing through human/spirit growth.
No need to ask what that will mean to spirit. It is spirit. You
are spirit.

No here. No there.

You are not a broken human there. Holes and wounds
provide divine lessons in the power of love, importance of
connection, presence of spirit. These are difficult ideas for
human incarnation, yet the potential for soul grown is
enormous.

Our gift to you—a gift of divine
love in the form of insight.

Divinely inspired.

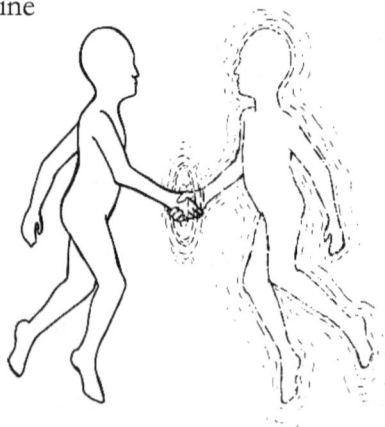

Origins
Reading 29

The human in you feels alone. The divine in you is not.

Good loving afternoon,

We have been asked to talk about your origins and connections and disconnection and those of all humanity. Understand the complexity of this. It will not be easy to grasp.

For you are an energy speck in a vast pulsing, teaming orb of energy—one of many. All unique in creation, yet all tied with a common filament of light to the divine. The scope is vast—far wider than you have imagined in your small, human, earthbound lens.

Your spark is infinite in its connection to the infinite. You are here now, so as you live it out, that defines the parameters of your concern. So hyper-focused on mother, children, job, home. What does all that mean?

It means while you are human, it is everything, but when you leave it is nothing except the changes to the energy wrought by your concerns.

The divine is the source of all—you were birthed from that— then your connection to it remained, but expanded as tendrils outward—wrapping around others, embracing soul forces around you.

In different incarnations you became a life form and the vast array of universal possibilities shape and expand you as all life experiences present themselves. While an incarnation, there are challenges; while in spirit, there are also challenges.

Go back to no here/there. Incarnation/spirit all one, sequentially delineated by location and circumstances. But there is no definitive division—ever—human/spirit, earth/heaven, you/me, good/evil, human/divine. All one. All ways.

Throw all of these together as same—different times, different places, different forms, different lessons, different pain. All the while the same spirit connection to the divine, connection to universal spirit of all, one, others.

So, why are some incarnations so....

See here, we get beyond the comprehension. We are struggling to explain because you are struggling to ask.

The fact you are asking why you are so different is an earthly question with a celestial answer, one you keep shutting down because you worry people will judge you harshly for writing our message.

In simple terms, you are different because you are a unique human/spirit incarnation. The questions you have always asked, the things you have always known, are the result of your unique creation and while we are all linked through energy and all linked to the divine, we are all different, so the way we live out our incarnations is different. We learn differently because we live differently, because our innate spirit was created through divinity as you—divinely connected, divinely created.

One of a kind yet linked to all.

So, while your goal there may be to understand your earthly struggles, you will be best served if you see them as spiritual as well. Your earthly self is the same as your spiritual self. Your earthly damage same as your spiritual damage.

The more you allow yourself to see, accept these truths, the more both earthly incarnation and spirit can heal and grow.

It matters naught if others believe or accept it. Each incarnation does its own dance to divine chords that chime throughout the universe.

If your paths cross, see both earthly and spiritual in others and in you.

Your disconnect this time is the result of your incarnation with others who are grandly out of sync with your spiritual path.

We would like to point out all that profound understanding that has come from that divinely inspired 'mistake'. Your spiritual growth this time is vast—so many complex ideas have entered your consciousness—such a blessing!

Quest defines you as human/spirit. Although you believe you have longed for greater adventures, this one was by far the grandest one a soul can undertake, so before you condemn yourself for your earthly pain and your small life, pause to return to that place in the universe where the divine energy embraces you and all others.

Few get to feel that while incarnated, so human/spirit painfully divided and human pain persists in body and spirit. You can move beyond that if you dare grasp what you know to be true, without fearing what people will think about you. Such an earthly concern.

Earthly pain is real. Earthly chains are not. Once you have felt the embrace of the universe, what does it matter what the human spirits around you believe? It matters naught to you what path they have chosen for their own spiritual incarnation.

Humanity is merely one incarnation of many possible. Spirit life is so much bigger than that.

Be fearless in your convictions and you will thrive in your spirit growth.

Human and spirit are united. The finite and the infinite reside together. Appreciate each for its purpose. See both. Accept both. Live both. Embrace both.

Now replace 'both' with 'one'. Both = one.

The human in you feels alone. The divine in you is not.

Earth
Reading 30

Fearlessly embrace earth as the dark pathway to enlightened love.

Good morning! We have been waiting for you. Today's topic—Earth!

You are here.

Here you have chosen to place your spirit in a body for the time being. It is very short-lived, yet important work.

What people forget is they are spirit residing in small body—not body with spirit as small part residing within.

Body takes on too much importance. It is a vessel you have chosen which is merely one path among many to grow spiritually. Yet, it comes with blinders—blinders that impede our insight into our emotions and wounds that require attention to foster spirit.

But that is the point. See?

This body, those emotions. They are vehicles to transform spirit—catalysts, as it were, to address deeper spiritual questions of connection and love.

If we stayed in spirit, how would we grow? Life in spirit is not perfect, but so much of learning connected to experience. Clarity and understanding while in spirit limiting in its own way.

Spirit tries to see/know clearly and yet—there is so much more to the divine that they fail to see. Divine created spirit and incarnations to complement each other in path to growth.

In spirit, clarity diminishes struggles and questions. You have learned it, so you can be complacent about the boundless capacity for divine power of love and connection.

Humans come here fully equipped with the built-in struggles of time and place that plague all humanity—from physical struggles of survival to emotional growth from situation. Each is special for its time and place and struggle.

Our biggest struggle here is to grasp full expanse of spirit and divine love. All search for that. Some attempts are organized faith practices, religious fanaticism, human-bound efforts to explain higher power beyond themselves and ease pain of loneliness and fear of life after death by imposing earth-bound rules on vast universal matrix.

Others fail to see it at all, become fully engulfed in human pain and try to bury the truth of pain in self-medication or creating archives on closely guarded shelves surrounded by thick walls, protecting us from discovery and each other.

All trying to heal wounds to strengthen ties to divine love, but all immersed in struggle/love balance. A dance between human and divinity that brings you here.

Trouble not over perceived failure to fully live in moment of human or gracefully dance to the divine music while here. Recognize the beauty of the dance and the power of link between the two—appreciate both are truly one in same.

Pain/love/growth/healing/love/stumble/love . . . one, two, three . . . one, two three . . .

Music—imagine music of the divine dance and you will hear it in your head and envision it in your heart. You are all waltzing through time, linked to one another, a combination of dancing spirit and current incarnation.

Envision the universe filled with life, teeming with energy, orchestrated with melodious harmony. Some in body are stumbling in darkness with spirit shrouded, some gliding to chords, some are partners of spirit and incarnation united and some currently spirit—all enjoy the echoes of celestial music that pulses through them with love.

Why take on the struggle of darkness and struggle with incarnation?

The universe if filled with opposites as you have seen. Light/Dark. Recognize the paradoxical nature of all things. It is through darkness we grow in appreciation for the warmth of light. It is through light that darkness is dispelled. Light/Dark.

Fearlessly embrace earth as the dark pathway to enlightened love. Darkness/Light. Human/Spirit.

It is _life_.

Life is here and there—it is one entwined vine that becomes stronger in connection.

Words fail in the attempt to convey grand nature of tapestry of universal life. Life is spirit and human. Life is one. Live it as such.

How do I do that?

Ah . . . moot question/answer really. Whether you want to—or not. Aren't you doing that already? Aren't you all?

Degree of seeing and hearing and embracing vary. Advice—open all senses to all connections human and spirit. Truth and love will enable you to see, hear, feel, touch, taste, experience life in all its glorious facets.

Enough for now.

Journey to ponder earthly incarnation. Continue on that path. Fully embrace pathway to divine in all its darkness—and its light.

One.

Heart Song 2- Heal

True Nature
Reading 1

Unearth your pure spirit.

If you ask, answer is explained through metaphor, paradox and characters.

Humans try to grasp the cosmic, but that must be explained in human terms to fit into small space of human reality. You are given many earthly references to understand the humanly incomprehensible and make vast scope comprehensible.

How to understand True Nature and True Healing? Are you true hard or veneer hard? Are you true soft or veneer soft? Who are you, really? What really lies at soul depth, masked by human limits, experiences, circumstances and responses?

To discover true nature, examine construction metaphor. In times of examination, work can be done behind the façade. The hammers bang. The saws make their cuts. Structures are built and altered if you open to change both surface and beneath. What renovations await those willing to give it a try? Veneers stripped away. Innate beauty exposed.

Construction, however, is not easy. Not quick. Not clean.

Construction is required to deal with the hardest of all—the wounds that morph into mysterious sink holes that threaten to engulf us without warning, the damage done beneath and behind. Oh, so easy to discuss the façade. To repair the façade. To beautify the pretty picture covering the circumstantial problems created by ignoring the reality of the damage. When we begin sinking, we can shore up the façade enough for now.

We think we can only go so far into the pain. We stop on the doorstep and shrug. It looks fine now. It hurts too much to look. The pain is too much, so we turn away and continue to ignore the real problem that keeps us from healing. Events we cannot discuss. The beloved and flawed people who caused the damage 'did their best', so what is to see? What if they didn't or couldn't or wouldn't—or really did?

Those who initiated the wounds (parents, siblings, relatives, friends, lovers, children) are left out of the narrative. They present the reason we cannot peer too intently into the hole. If we do, then what? Dance around it, we do.

But.

It is possible to love them and still repair the hole, unearth your pure spirit. You don't have to give up protection and denial to heal. It is not even necessary to forgive. Just accept the way it is in all its flaws and complexity. To be healed must allow the good, the bad and the ugly to reside in paradox. No one is asking you to give the people or feelings away. Expand them to include a fuller picture of what reality was then and what it is now.

Multidimensional. All facets part of accepted reality. Pain . . . √. Love . . . √. All facets merely are. Healing just embraces the paradox and allows true spirit to emerge safely to survey and live amid dark and the light. It will always be part of you, earthly and spirit entwined. Accept both as one.

We are sparks of light, life as it spins through the paradox— facets, shifting, exposed.

All exist at same time—take center stage at different times and different experiences.

Circumstances present themselves. We respond with what we have constructed in the hard and soft veneers, to protect and preserve the holes and wounds.

Construction projects of soul nature can heal and renovate spirit in ways vividly colored with healing. We have invested much in protecting holes from further damage but have also preserved them in ways that allow them to bring shade to our lives.

As sparks of light, do not dim the possibility of spirit through maintenance of veneer. Address paradox of darkness of hole and healing of light. Let both exist. No veneer necessary as true spirit comes to fruition.

Melding Opposites
Reading 2

We are unique spirits at one with wholly divine.

Good morning child,

We have been waiting, toes tapping impatiently—so much to say!

Well, we understand your pacing. So many balls in the air, juggling not easy.

You are right to sense construction, but don't forget us! We are an integral part of the process—insight given to you to illuminate for you and for others.

Eager to begin Song 2.

First, consider the last entry. You questioned origins of you vs. us. It was your construction being brought to light. Repairing holes, earthly and important for melding human and spirit, but not spirit message for all necessarily.

So, with that, today's topic—melding. Interesting word, yes?

You have been noticing what you call paradox—opposites next to each other that are true—you seem to be able to see both and accept seeming contradiction in truth.

Next challenge—can you see them as one?

All those opposites you see, all those compartments for isolation and separation are not really an apartment facility with separate storage compartments for differing, contradictory views.

All barriers have to melt down.

Ultimate road to acceptance is to let all flow into same deep well of existence:
Past, present, future—one.
You and others—one.
Human and spirit—one.
Even walls of sink hole metaphor you like, those separations do not exist.

In reality, all one. You are envisioning a swirling pool of energy, filled with water mixing, mingling, swirling, dark. How does that metaphor work? What does it mean for you?

Gaze at the pool and just watch barriers dissolve.

It is you now, but also in past bodies and forever soul, surrounded by past lives and past experiences in this life and all experiences in all lives.

So here you are in this moment but strive to see it in its totality. All that is past, spirit and human—all that is now, this life, past, future desires. So it is with you and all others.

Can that view be expanded to remove the boundaries that separate your experience into compartments and apply that to all other spirits/people as well?

Next biggest challenge—expand the scope and see the vast intermingling of souls, lives, divine—all one.

Ultimate cosmic challenge—we are unique spirits at one with wholly divine and all its energies in all its oneness.

Talk about paradox!

You are trying to envision how to meld unique within vastly one. Envision the pool and you in it. The walls separating do not disappear. Instead, they transform into lines of strong connection—there, but not there—energy bonds that link, but do not separate. It is a woven tapestry of one that is beautiful, unique fibers within, yet indistinguishable from one another when whole beauty is appreciated.

The true paradox lies in the scope of the unique spark of you in the grand vista of infinity; these two are not separate, nor indistinguishable—they are one.

To heal self to live authentically in body and spirit, you must grasp this overriding idea that it all needs to meld together and it all needs to make sense without effort on a soul/ universal level. Opposites do not exist side by side as in paradox; perhaps they are not opposites at all.

Keep stressing one. Not opposites at all. See one. The construction you hear is not necessarily building but deconstructing those false notions of separation.

Pain, hurt, protection, voices all built out of separation. True strength comes in pulling down scaffolding to see oneness. Beauty and growth from pain. Evolution of self over several planes.

Happiness in acceptance of what is. Strength in accepting human weakness and flaws melded with pure authentic spirit.

Enough for now about melding. It is a big topic, one of the biggest. More to be revealed as human mind and heart and awareness expand with deconstruction of earthly barriers that limit understanding to only that which we can see in pinprick lens of body.

Always amazing, isn't it?

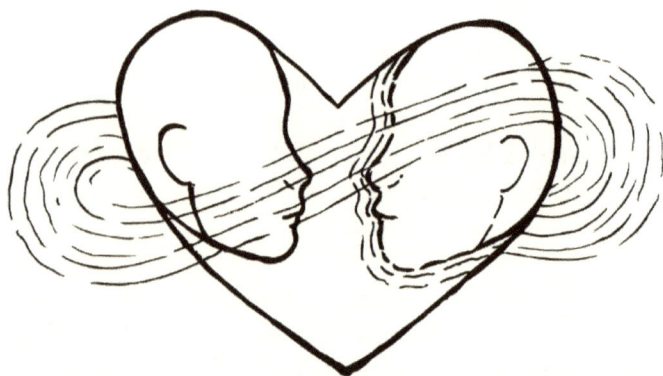

Cosmic Patience
Reading 3

When healing wounds, you are really searching to honor your true spirit.

Buenos Dias!

Getting into right mind important—for you. We wait patiently as you progress in your engagement with us, not with cosmic laughter, but with cosmic patience.

Cosmic patience—ponder that as today's thought.

So much of life is mired in impatience. It seems to move you ahead faster, facilitates movement forward. But does it? Really?

That rush you feel is human. You must use your body to DO SOMETHING and things will get better. You are convinced movement 'forward' = better. It will fix problems, make progress.

Envision the scope, however. It is so much larger. See the scene before you with sparks of life/light, connections to grander schemes, patterns, being.

Paradox today—can false movement forward really just be expansion of light here and now in space occupied by spirit—in body or not—human or energy? Could it just be the expansion of connection to each other and to the divine?

Even progression of human incarnation (life) not movement, just expansion or not to varying degrees.

If you can envision your spirit light, watch it expand and contract, glow and dim, join with others or disconnect, flow or stop—without movement forward.

Progress is human construct to explain decisions, changes, aging. Much human thought is an effort to learn more about the divine with blinders on. Divine is too great to comprehend for spirits or humans, so think of human incarnations as baby's first wobbly steps—stumbling to move, unplanned, really, just preparing for the joys of discovery on meandering paths filled with stumbles, escapes, races, tripping over our feet as we try to vault to joyful freedom.

Making a decision—leaving, staying, moving—no different in spirit/human for progression than seeing joy in the beautiful sunset or sensing the pure divinity in a baby's hug.

Reexamine forward push, healing 'progress'. Focus on now. How is now expanding? How does finding divine in moment feel? Does a decision help or hinder expansion of spirit in time and place?

There you are, a pulsing light. Let it flood into your consciousness as human. As humans, we focus on forward of human and deny development of spirit and its strong and beautiful oneness with human incarnation.

When healing wounds, you are really searching to honor your true spirit. Something earthly has injured and buried that. When you peer into the hole beyond the pain, you are envisioning authentic spirit looking up at you, waiting patiently to be discovered.

It is cosmic patience. It has all the time in the universe because it is timeless. It is not worried it will be found. If not now, next time. It knows it will flourish when you see it and honor it because it is essentially you and you recognize the purity and value of your own spirit when you see it.

If, as a human, you can unearth and discover and honor your authentic spirit self, then you may also recognize the place and power in cosmic patience.

Be brave. Find the wounds. Peer into the darkness of the hole. See for the first time the pure nature of your spirit self. Smile and reach out your hand to help it into the joyful everyday of your current incarnation—and don't forget to thank it for waiting—and for sharing the gift of cosmic patience.

Unfiltered Love
Reading 4

Dwell in heart center—always and everywhere.

Hello darling,

Glad to see you today, as always. We suggest you open before sitting to join us. No worries about connection. It is there. We are with you and will come.

Today's topic—unfiltered love.

We sense your hesitation as you ponder that. Where did that come from, you ask.

It lies patiently in your heart center—the center of all that is life. You have been told over and over and over that love reigns supreme in life and spirit power. It is relational. It describes your connection to the divine, to spirit life, to other spirits, to your own spirit and to other humans. Now you see where this is going.

If pure, unfiltered love is the primary tenant of spirit, why such a struggle while human?

Spirit struggle is inherently different while in that incarnation, but why?

While in spirit, we recognize connections to other spirits, life force and divine, but that world is so limited in its potential for growth, as problems often foster growth. We know that as humans because our struggles offer us ample opportunity for growth. While in spirit you can bask in connection and understand all, but where is the challenge? All conflict is hypothetical opportunity, but in spirit, frailty and vulnerability limited; so is that which fosters struggle steeped in paradox.

It isn't that spirit doesn't have remnants of humanity, but remember, truly human experience fraught with intellect vs. emotional balance and struggle—the paradox! Spirit life lacks the tension of paradox that challenges us to see that opposites can be true and live harmoniously.

Remember the discussion of paradox? Unique vs. vastly one. Movement forward vs. expansion in place. Earthly vs. spiritual. How to reconcile all opposites?

As humans, we feel goal/demand is to choose one side, focus, always move forward.
Where is the acceptance of totality in that? Life should encompass truthful study and acceptance of paradox—life is not black and white or even gray.

Paradox allows that there are more than two contradictions. A whole spectrum of life exists and those contradictions are not that. They are merely flashes of colors that sometimes bump up against each other and appear opposite, but truly aren't.

Which brings us back to today's message—unfiltered love. See these paradoxes as human filters designed to challenge and refine our view and interactions with each other as humans and spirits with links to the divine. Human eyes are filtered eyes. Our vision is clouded with struggle so we can learn to see. Paradox forces us to look through the human lens. If we see merely black and white, the lens is human. If we see bursts of color, we are allowing spirit in. If we grow in spirit and can accept the contradictions and struggles really aren't, we may see nothing but one—love unfiltered. This is divine love, untainted by human filters.

Your thoughts are all tumbling around. This idea that is so hard to grasp and yet so simple in its clarity of one idea. Our connection to the divine is love. Our connection to other spirits is love. Our connection to our own spirit is love. Our connection to other humans, believe it or not, is also love. In all cases, one vast system of energy connected through pulsing streams. It is not accident that love is our biggest challenge on earth. It is the most distorted lens we are given. The emotions and intellect inherent in human body experience create this challenge.

So how to use human to grow in spirit?

Work to see and understand the tensions. Work to see the challenges they present. See those challenges as pathways to true love. See that love as central to our human/spirit lives.

Unfiltered love will expand your soul beyond the wildest expectations of limited human vision. Expand your perceptions to contemplate connections of human . . . to paradox . . . to spirit . . . to unfiltered love . . . to one.

Such truth in contradiction! Ha!

Push beyond the filters.
See beyond the lens.
Embrace the immensity of paradox.
Accept all that is—
       Unfiltered—
        As one—
        Love—

Dwell in heart center—always and everywhere.

Heart Songs

You are an integral musician in the cosmic tune.

Good morning.

Today's date is locational in time and space—a mere dot in the continuum. Here you are present at this ongoing moment in time—and as you write this, it has moved on from when you have started—all changed, all the same— another paradox for you to contemplate.

So here you are again today, hoping to connect for enlightenment. We want to remind you we are always there. These are the only times you offer your hand for the purpose of sharing, so while it would seem you are waiting for us to show up, it is we who are waiting for you to become available for this—though the order does not really matter.

Let us stop dancing around today. This infinite message is for this moment in this time.

Today, our ideas center around heart song—the vibration of truth that emanates from your heart-centered soul and echoes through infinity into the heart centers of other spirits and humans and serves as a primary thread that courses from the divine to all other souls.

You can envision this, of course, through many metaphors— the arteries and veins that course through you. The cycles of the climate that nourish the earth. The delicate balance in the universe we cannot comprehend—even the vast interconnection between the earth, the sun and the moon that governs all life here.

Interestingly, the sun and moon seem to derive nothing from this relationship—and earth derives everything.

What of that?

Perhaps that is a good metaphor for the spirit/human/divine connection.

The sun is blazing with power and energy, contributing in ways beyond human comprehension. But just because we fail to understand it does not mean it isn't there; it just means while here we have limits to our connections that we struggle to understand.

Perhaps full understanding of spirit power is too grand, too 'hot," too much for us in human form. But that, other than respectfully studying and acknowledging, is not our main focus.

Our main focus here is our design as humans, where our role seems to be to learn to survive, study and take from the power that is spirit and perhaps appreciate the warmth of that heart center—and accept we may never understand, while here, what spirit gains from this seemingly one-sided relationship.

What does spirit provide to us that we are doomed to fully grasp while in human form?

The power of warmth, the power of unreciprocated connection. It provides heart strength in ways unbidden and unwavering in powerful waves of energy that flow to us.

Such as it is with heart songs. If you could hear the power of that connection, the pulsing of that energy, what would it sound like?

Right now you hear the earthly—the cars, the birds. But what if you could hear the cosmic? The pulses of warmth, the unwavering and unreturned waves of the divine enter you as human through your heart. HOW DIVINE WOULD THAT MUSIC BE?

And yet it is always there, playing away beyond your ears because they often provide blockage to your heart. But if you pause and seek your heart-center, you may not hear the song of this connection, but you could perhaps feel it. Yes, you can feel it now as it fills you with power and wonder. Admire this moment.

Even if you as human-limited fail to see how earth benefits the sun, know that your tuning into heart song strengthens you in spirit and reinforces your connection to the divine that is unwavering and loving beyond human measure.

Bask in this warm connecting flow to and from your heart. Perhaps what you should seek to hear most is how you are an integral musician in the cosmic tune. It is indeed a flow that goes both ways and is not independent of one another.

No.

In cosmic music, all instruments play a role, yours, too. Yours especially if you are seeking to understand great orchestration in the divine aria.

One. Again.

All the hearts, all the humans, all the spirits, all connected. All individual while all being one, playing in the band of cosmic reverie. Grand thought, isn't it? Take a peek into that beating heart and see if you can't find the thread of the connection to the divine—and to each other.

Then listen carefully as the music soothes all souls and soul connections to ease pain, enable growth. Expand beyond your lack of understanding of cosmic connection reflected in the sun and earth, human/spirit and divine.

All!

The music is already playing.
Let your awareness of it begin!
The heart song plays on in you.

Beyond and Within
Reading 6

Your spirit is yearning for reconciliation.

Good morrow and salutations. We have waited patiently, and here we are.

So much continues to go on with you—steps forward, steps back, steps open . . . steps like a dance to divine music, orchestrated beyond and within your grasp.

As are most things. Beyond and within—next paradox to consider.

How often do we walk that tightrope, trying to bring the beyond within our grasp while we are in human incarnation? Ah, look at all the bridges designed to do that: metaphors, paradoxes, ideas spiritual designed as human, all that embedded in human experience and understanding.

Today consider psychology/spirit. Religion/spirit. Familial relationships/spirit. Back to question of here vs. there. All are one, but because humans are 'gifted' with earthly struggles and emotions, their vision of spirit is vastly dimmed in them, shrouded by limits of brain/emotions/intellect/ego. You keep using that / to delineate. Try to imagine life without the /.

Humans are learning that brains and emotions are not so strongly separated as they would like to believe. Perhaps sociological religion not so 'spiritual' after all. Human behavior is so driven by forces unseen and not understood and yet no one looks to spirit for answers.

Humans look to science to explain part of human brain that controls emotions in unseen ways. And yet to know your heart's heart, shall you look in your brain for explanation?

It is true there is connection between human and emotion, but that is exploring the wrong direction. You seem able to accept that human behaviors are complex in connected ways and want to see the answer on a CT scan.

But maybe this / of division between brain and emotion, action and perception, is just another way humans are struggling to understand concepts beyond their limited scope of understanding. Instead of widening the lens, you are just digging around, trying to the connect the known to the known, as if that will give you answers to the unknown.

If you can accept that humans of intellect are driven by emotional forces unseen, why can't you accept humans of intellect and emotion seeking spiritual forces unseen?

While we come here to learn and humanness facilitates that, we are also here to grow. Ignoring spirit while here may facilitate learning but may not foster growth.

To flourish as human incarnation in spirit, you must dissolve that line that you always use to separate the apparent, but false paradox relationship.

In spirit we are human; as humans we are also in spirit.

Seeing and embracing spirit is to return to whole—see more, grow more, accept more—

Touching and accepting spirit is reaching out to see yourself in greater depth—a 3D experience designed to heal the rift that artificially divides each and all.

In human, a curtain is dropped between body and spirit. While here, you are engulfed in sights, sounds, emotions. And yet, if you peer carefully behind the curtain, into what seems to be darkness (but is really light), you will grasp a brilliance and a being so grand in completeness. Do not look to your brain for peace. Do not look to religious rules for guidance. Do not examine CT scan to give you answers to the mysterious and the divine.

The answers are in you through the conduit of the heart— your spirit is yearning for reconciliation. The true challenge of humanity is not to seek the answers to heal humanity from without—the answers are within, linked through the tunnel of heart light that links you to your spirit and to the divine and to all other spirits.

Ironically, the darkness does not exist on the other side of the curtain. The mystery is not there. The mystery is here and you flounder to explain it in so many ineffective ways.

In reality, our charge here is to deconstruct that false line and allow the light of spirit to enlighten the shadows of humanity.

All humans are merely fumbling around to find the light switch to divine light. This is challenging at night, but as in all metaphors, you know the connection is real and the switch can be flipped—and the light can flow in.

Hint: the light switch is in your heart in case the metaphor got away from you. Click!

Darkness is not dispelled by getting directions about how to install the switch (religion), or learning how a light switch works (science), or trying to understand why the light switch doesn't seem to want to turn on (psychology).

Find heart center. Click it.

Look within to peer beyond.

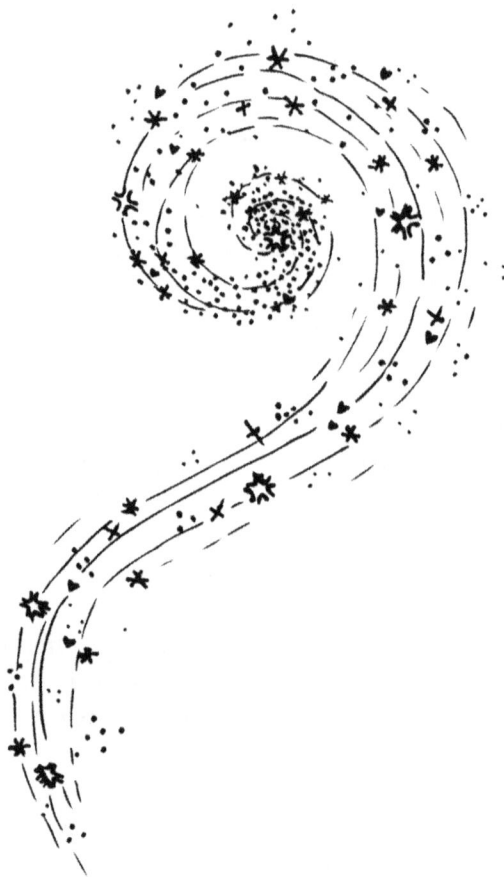

Soul Decisions
Reading 7

Spiritual decisions are made in search of authenticity.

Good morning. I greet you with great happiness—so much to say—yet respectful of boundaries you have set.

Today's message—sharing souls or soul intersection. You are so roiled by the idea of connection and separation, which is a paradox of one, yet not one. How to be human incarnation and spirit all at once? And how to be connected to all spirits of universal energy and being and yet so you at the same time? It is all in how you see boundaries. Do they separate or link? Are you more linked without a boundary? Or does link still exist?

Contemplate the metaphor of a fence. The fence exists. It is a boundary between two territories—yours and mine. But if you take an aerial view of the fence, it is all part of a landscape much bigger and if you remove it, that does not make boundaries vanish. Boundaries exist in the form of flesh and wood and concrete—and air and choices.

Just as you have separation in human form, you have separation in spirit form, but just because you separate does not mean you are not connected. There are all sorts of connections; familial, spiritual, friendship, acquaintances, colleagues—spirit.

But we have set boundaries in all of them. So even spiritually you can set parameters larger than you thought. That does not negate the fact you remain connected. The fence still exists and yet you remain linked.

Feeling alone illustrates your soul's setting of parameters. What makes you think that just because you feel alone that you are to blame or that you are in essence disconnected? Stop thinking in the terms that here I am isolated, but there all of that goes away, or that people here who experience great connection to others don't also feel the paradox of connection/isolation when in human or in spirit.

Stop thinking earthly life is terrible and as spirit you will laugh at your human frailties with pure insight and healing.

First: We have said no true here or there. You straddle both always. There is no finite separation housed strictly in body—you are spirit in both places although your physical parameters vary. Experiences human/not human are different it is true, but while not human the physical restrictions are different, but your authentic spirit remains throughout.

You do not come here with painful, distorting blinders on to facilitate growth. Growth in spirit is spirit—in different times, in different dimensions, in different incarnations; it is authentic self, working toward insight and enlightenment.

Same/different. Same/different. Same different. The ultimate paradox of the spirit.

You can be connected with others, but you set the parameters. You can be human/spirit, but you can close the door to insight and focus the lens only on that which you experience at the moment. You can be connected to others, spirit or human, but you can also build fences.

If there are repetitions, recurrences, there are reasons. If you isolate yourself while human, when, how, why are there fences? Fences always exist, but why do they exist as boundaries, isolators rather than connectors?

Why the boundaries so fortified? All within your spiritual jurisdiction, not for blame purposes, but for yearning, speculation, long view. What, perhaps, is the spiritual decision to place yourself in fortress of 'wrong' place?

Blame is a very human response that should be banished from vocabulary. Spiritual decisions are made in search of authenticity, not as punishment or karma or vengeance.

Search for recognition, appreciation, understanding, insight into spiritual decisions in quest for reaching toward the divine. They are your unique spiritual decisions in your very own quest. Which means you must stop measuring your soul journey to others' soul journeys. Comparison of journeys is misplaced energy at best and damaging to soul at worst.

Rise above the view from the ground where fences box you in. Envision the freedom of seeing from above, how all energy flows and is connected and fences exist, but not to wall off and end the search or kill the soul.

We know they fail as defensive measures. The Great Wall failed miserably. What good can come of creating boundaries?

Be careful they do not enclose you. They can provide the distance and lack of intrusion to see without interruption. Respect the soul decisions you have made in your own search for authentic soul growth.

The walls that separate also connect and they are not worthy of fortress status as effective blockers. Take the ride above to see how they fit into the journey as insulation that serves to warm and protect, but not separate or harm.

How can these separations exist at the same time as interconnections? You have created space to examine such weighty issues. It is a soul's decision to seek and experience true challenges in quest for divine light.

All things can be seen in many ways. Time to reexamine your view of separation/connection and your authentic soul self.

We all establish our little patch of space to sow our garden of self-development. Look at your garden. Tend to it for enlightenment. Accept it. Nurture it. See how it is both separate from others and part of the cosmic.

Purposefully unfettered.

Accept Now
Reading 8

The candy tastes delicious in your mouth.

Good morning,

Life goes by, does it not? Remember, though, linear thinking is earthly thinking, so all those lines you draw in time and space are false, process thinking.

<u>NOW</u> is all there is.

The past no longer exists—or exists only as vapors of the energetic known as memories. The future only exists as a thought you wish would happen . . . and planning is so based on the vapors of the past and clouded now.

So, you wait for something to happen—when it is happening now—the only place where anything truly happens. The only moment that truly exists is right now—so morning questions should be, what to do now.

Much of life is clouded by skewed memories that do not exist any longer and events down the road that may or may not happen. There you have the fallacy of human thought—that you can keep the past alive and vibrant the way you wish it had happened (that is how you have catalogued it) and the future that may or may not become real.

What happens now? What is the value of now?

Right now is the moment in which you truly live and yet it does not take center stage because you are always preparing for what you are going to do next: throughout the day, throughout life, throughout eternity . . . all very pleasant pastimes in dreaming, but not real.

The sense of now is tied to the elusive 'acceptance' which you claim to seek 'in the future.' If only I could accept . . . I hope to find out what acceptance means . . . I could/would heal and go on better, happier, stronger.

See. You are banking on happiness by waiting for something to happen—the 'if only—in the future I hope' is so FUTURE.

It is staring you in the face. If you live right now, you accept.

You know the past holds no power over you because it is gone. Although it lives in your spirit, it is only as real and powerful as you allow.

And the future is oh, so, maybe/possible/not real/not there/imagined/hoped.

It is now that lies unrecognized for its acceptance and its beauty. You are constantly focused on untangling the past in order to improve the future. See what is missing? You have invested all your energy in past and future. You believe if only you could unmask one you could find happiness in the other.

Right here, right now is the only gift you have been given and yet you ignore it by disregarding its power.

Acceptance of now requires serious shift of your energy and does not negate your connection to others—in the now—and the beyond—in the now. All exist here and there and everywhere in the now.

You can look at the past, but not as a key to a happy future. It exists as an archive and should be treated as such, as an interesting record of what happened, but it is only as valuable as you make it.

Humans want to know the future because it makes them feel safe, but deep down you know it is totally incomprehensible and unpredictable. You could die in two minutes, you could make some investments, you could live well, you could get sick. Much of which has nothing to do with what you are doing at this moment, such as writing this from us to you.

What is acceptance? Now is now. It is the most valuable asset you have. It is life in this form right this minute and nothing more. You can plan, but realize the heart of that is futility, and a shift of focus from now.

It makes you feel a bit better, fine. Just recognize its limited scope and potential detriments.

Your charge—Try living now. Recognize use of energy to reminisce or hope. We have said it before.

Connect this—You are here. It is what it is. Acceptance is now.

Plan accordingly—Ha! Just joking!

Take your breath. Feel your body. Absorb your world. Your soul spark exists now. It is beautiful. It is your life. It is your gift—now.

The candy tastes delicious in your mouth. Not in the photo of you eating it as a child or on the shelf in the store before you buy it.

Life. Same thing.

Human Cha-Cha
Reading 9

Take on the weight of the body to expand the flight of the spirit.

Hallelujah and hello.

Welcome to the land of energy and spirit—connected one, connected all, connected here, connected there. One. All one.

We welcome the time you tune into the connection, though you must know you are connected whether you take pause to see it or not. When you want or need it, we are here. You are the limiting factor in current form on earth in human incarnation, struggling to be one amid flood of all the darkness humanity entails.

Emotion lies at the center of human experience. It colors your world. It shapes your soul growth. Incarnated it is sharp, raw, influential—a distinction from when in spirit. It is all about that brain and the physical points that come in the human body that do not always govern spirit forms with such strength.

That world is governed by the body; complex, beautiful, weak, flawed and vulnerable—limited in its scope and span.

It is restrictive, but don't forget oh, so liberating as well. It allows you to inhabit a rich sensory vista of intense experiences—tied to others in order to waltz through a lifetime, which means inherent bumps and clashes as two and more incarnations bump around trying to manage the hallmarks of the physical incarnation; illness, relationship, proximity, emotion—a stew of liberty and restriction, a beautiful paradox of challenge that gives spirit a rich opportunity to exist in a physical experience.

Of course, spirit has its own unique ways, too. Without body its existence is entirely different, yet so similar in many ways. Without the physical, the focus is on that which we merely glimpse here—spiritual development and freedom. Yet without body that incarnation takes on its own way of existence, a state humans are not privy to see. It is you in a different form, to have different experiences of connection— spiritual always, human sometimes and guess what? There are more ways and more opportunities than you can imagine.

When in any form, you are limited by state of your situation. When human, limited yet enabled by body and the earth. When spirit, limited by lack of body, but enabled by freedom from that, too.

We have used word pinprick. As human incarnation, you can only grasp a pinprick of the reality of spirit because you are there to be intensely focused on human experience on earth.

You really only peer through a small pinpoint of light to grasp spirit while there. Yes, you have seen the expanse and marveled at the connection and even stepped suspended into the void of the vast universe, but that is not spiritual life when not human. It is far more complex and different than you can conceive. So, while it is nice to float in the awesome expanse of universal energy, in truth you are experiencing right now as human—and should revel in the moment of that experience—darkness, pain, love, light, dance, art, promises, hugs, fears—all of it beautiful and all valuable. Even in its pain there is connection and growth and value beyond words.

Your time there is short. Best possible lesson is to live it all. Feel it all. Doesn't mean just test the waters, live dangerously or give in to the dark. It means savor its intensity. Dance while you can. Sing while you have vocal chords. You thought you would be free after death and could sing all you wanted—and we asked you why to wait until then? Remember. Don't wait until then. What awaits is different and the cha-cha of clashing limbs and lives takes on a whole new way to be. When you peered through the dark and saw the expanse, did you see bodies dancing around? You did not!

You really shouldn't wait until you leave your body to enjoy the 'freedom' you couldn't have there. That is missing the entire point of choosing incarnation—to take on the weight of the body to expand the flight of the spirit.

So much truth in contradiction! Time and bodies both restrictive but offer opportunity for rich growth. Use both to take joy in the breath on earth—the existence of you—in whatever form you live at the moment.

Always flip the coin to the other side. Flip the coin that is small and flat to open the door to the vast and incomprehensible. Value all. Live now. Savor beauty—even when shaded with pain or complication or frustration. Grasp the paradox. Feel today's body. Live timeless spirit.

In all planes, there is feeling the truth, but not all truth comes in words.

Contemplate a vast expanse beyond human words and that may help you value your current place as part of the finite within the infinite—and value the beauty of all existences as a spirit connected to divine splendor beyond comprehension.

Uniquely You
Reading 10

You are you—that little child born into the world was soul as is.

Welcome to new ideas and an open mind. We missed you, so it good to see you return. Welcome child of questions seeking answers.

Today, we shall talk about you—the center of all acceptance, worst critic and best friend.

You have been struggling with acceptance and improvement—past, present and future elements—add to your senses.

There is only now.

There is only you. As is. That is acceptance. It does not preclude you from being happier. Just realize, you are not charged with changing you. You are you. It is what it is. You are charged with looking past to see how manifestation of you, social you, adapted to life forces and events, realizing they did not change you at all. They changed how you reacted to your life, how you responded to events, interacted with others, dealt with opportunities and challenges. Adapted to life as human, in body, on earth.

But you? You are you—that little child born into the world was soul as is—and then life began to be a series of adaptation and compromises. Your adult behavior is merely how you have adapted to the life lived. How did you protect yourself? How did you learn to take chances? Love? Try?

Keep in mind it is a grand dance between you and yourself. Souls are not the same and lives vary widely, so your adaptive behavior is uniquely you, forged with the heat of life, buffeted by the winds.

Acceptance is you looking at both elements—who you are in the heart and who you have become as a result of this life—one at this point. Key challenge is to discern the two and unify them to make now authentically healthy, peaceful and live as a soul in body, though both are one.

Life offers you the opportunity to respond in a myriad of ways and just because you have responded in the 'wrong' way, in a certain way, doesn't mean that has to continue. Which leads us to acceptance again. You cannot negate the forces that forged your responses or the changes to your behavior they wrought, but acceptance means you say, "Yes. Hey. Thanks. You did wonderfully well helping me adapt and stay safe. I know you aren't going anywhere. Speak your peace but know that I may not need you to protect me right at this moment."

Because acceptance means you know your responses in the past may have been necessary and may have prevented peace and happiness in ways unseen, but now is now. The winds may blow, but each moment offers opportunity for response. "Thank you, but it is better for me to do it this way, this time." Comforting and caressing all responses and making best selection in the now. Acceptance also means there is no pressure to select the 'right' one, the 'best' one', the 'healthiest' one. In the moment of now you are merely picking the one that makes the most sense as life happens.

You can strive to make those most authentic at the soul level, but do not berate yourself for going with the little human crouched in the corner of a wound. Perhaps a little protection is in order, so now accepts both in loving way—

open-armed, open-hearted to self, realizing those around you are needed and valued, but we are too hard on them and ourselves. You have already put into your consciousness the variety of ways that exist to respond, but you always applied that to your response to others, not kindness to self.

Soul self/human self are one and deserving of respect. You must work to see both, understand both as one. Forgive self for perceived failures and self-disappointments. Regret is often that failure to see self in loving, kind way, like you must at all times do what is best, right.

You have always lived in a moment whether you realized it or not and filled your place with past concerns (regrets) or hopes (future). Acceptance lives in now. Just because you have not always seen it that way does not mean you cannot in this moment and every other—and accept the wind is blowing. Your vision may be clouded. Your body hunkered down. Only choice is how to respond to the wind you cannot stop.

Life affirming? Dangerous?

Next moment coming . . . here now . . . only way to deal with self is acceptance. There will be wind. You will respond. Next moment here. Now what? Stop and breathe it in and decide, then watch the flow continue in the dance that is life—now. All you have been given.

Now is all you have.

Dance on. Some days the dance is better than others.

So what?

Reality Lit

Reading 11

It is your own light that illuminates the darkness.

Good day and happy occurrences!

Breathe. Feel the energy. We are here—always.

Interesting to watch the swirl as you ready to receive our message today—fear, apprehension, anticipation.

Light, how about light?

Oh, so many ways to embrace that word.
Light—meaning to feel less heavy, without weight.
Light—floaty, airy, above it all.
Light—What is needed to 'see' better.

We are the light bearers and you the candle incarnate. All these meanings combine in our purposes jointly. Our goal is to provide the light that sheds light on the weight of human to surround those who wish to embrace lightness of spirit— the insight, the balance to weight.

So, watch the candlelight flicker—much like humanity— when you choose to light it—when it flickers, struggling to solidify understanding of nature/spirit/human interaction. Just go with the heat, beauty and illumination spirit provides. That flickering light is not just without in earthly form. It is within in spirit form. Hot. Glowing. Leading a path out of darkness.

You have lived in holes of darkness, huddled trying to safely shield from winds of earthly. Envision having a candle there with you. You do, you know. You are the kindling and the flame and the heat and the glow, side-by-side and inside the darkness of hurt child.

Can you see both? Can be said light does not change the situation. It merely changes the view of the situation—what it looks like, what you can see. Child is still there. Hurt still there. But stumbling can be curtailed. Comfort taken. Insight gained in waves of light that do not change, but illumination allows better, more accurate view of earthly life.

Acceptance of dark hole/light juxtaposition key in comprehending human experience. Some people live in darkness because they do not know light exists. Some look around for outside source of light to lead them out of darkness. You do not need to exist darkly or wait for someone to show you the path out of it.

The light is in you—at all times! It is your own light that illuminates the darkness, your own divine. Fan the light within you. It is that which you have called 'health/healing' in human terms. Fan the flames of spirit in you and watch the glow expand, the flame flourish.

We are there to blow the winds with you and provide the peephole of light to lead you to your own enlightenment. Watch the flame flow from your heart and expand into the universe of connection to other souls and the divine and suddenly you are not alone in the dark.

Take comfort in the beyond human. It flickers. It puzzles. It is hard for the human mind/body to grasp. How can two be one? How can human nurture divine spark? How can pain exist next to such peace?

Remind yourself of so many things we have said before. All is one. You are connected to the divine through spirit.

Humanity is part dark and part light, part human and part spirit. You have power of light in you to see beyond world of darkness.

You are not a prisoner there! You have just failed to see because you are looking beyond the time and place to be rescued from darkness. How can that happen? Now is the only time that truly exists. The past is merely a chronology of events in your story. The future is ethereal. The only reality is now.

So, in the hole, only now exists. Humans try to mend/change/rewrite the past, but this is not possible. It is what it is. Trying to plan for the future is not possible. It simply doesn't exist.

Your challenge—how do you want to live NOW so the unknowable events of the future become a happy, healthy past? How to make now what you want it to be to create the future/soon to be past you desire? Now is, in truth, the only option you have.

Everyone just fails to see it because we bemoan the past and wish the future has a different outcome, but we forget now is key to flipping on the light, using our insight to understand past influences to improve actions now so our future becomes reality in a joyful way.

So much to consider—shape now to make future events look like the past we would like to have. Process that in your heart and your head, human.

Let the light wash over the past events to illuminate now—to shape what is to come with positive energy. In now dwells the light that dwells in you. We can use it to reflect past or guide our way to a future, but first we must light the darkness of human experience to join with spirit in now, which is really all you have.

Reality lit!

Let it glow, grow, expand, flourish and all phases in the continuum will benefit. Ah, words have such limits!

Continuum Matrix
Reading 12

Acceptance requires cutting down the brambles that life built around your heart.

Good morning. You made it! Just a few funny fits and starts to illustrate main idea before we begin today.

Nothing is concrete—nothing is truth that negates something entirely false. Both too hard to define/know. Such as human—are you self-contained vessel of brain, body, blood flowing? Then how to explain emotion which is linked to the intangible of heart? Are you a conduit of connected energy, merely here to share energy flow of others and divine in the universal matrix?

How can this be yes and no? Paradox again and again and again.

You can indeed be self-contained if you choose to be such. No acknowledgement of energy connection shuts down all of those connections to encourage only focus on human and earthly. Or, you can open the portals and feel that some connection exists. Very few humans are more energy connected to the divine than they are human. Look to these true spiritual leaders, not those manifested as human that guide their earthly emotions of greed, hate, suppression, exclusion. Pretense of spirit sleight of hand, more earthly than divine.

Side-by-side/in one/at the same time, it is possible to be just one or any combination—all on a continuum. The biggest idea is that often our place on the continuum is self-chosen— no, always chosen—in terms of our own visions and choices.

All these stumbles this morning illustrate a 'path'—stumble, stumble, focus, stumble, problem; so, see with human intellect, feel with heart, solve with spirit if you allow. All the humans around you—including you—all exist on the continuum, but realize it is no linear line. You may be here, you may be there. You may shift, divide, feel, see—connect to an energy that enlightens or choose a path with tunnel option only. Those around you are all over as well.

Perhaps continuum not the best word, but best we can offer from limited human vocabulary. Matrix better, but harder to see. You can be a spirit in light in this, but a human limit in that, so envision yourself and the nature of life in all its complexity, micro and macro. Light/dark, seeing/blindness, pain/joy, truth/paradox, knowing/mystery—not really opposites, though. Just sides of the dice, rays of the light both limited and enlightened all at once.

So, the point is to get to know authentic self, light and dark, in recognition of your true nature. All facets of your own paradox must be embraced, deciding how to live in the second you breathe is manifestation of this true self— sometimes your best self and sometimes not—sometimes light, connected self, oftentimes not. A breath infuses you with life and spirit infuses you with energy and taking a breath of life deliberately denotes acceptance of self. Yes, this is you—hello—live life as such.

Self-awareness and acceptance are really key here. Knowing and connecting to others inevitable, but not your primary purpose—so self-contained—and yet you draw the energy of existence from a bigger source and a connected source. That exists as power as well.

To know self is to use and accept paradox to live and love as own unique energy. Each breath is your own. Caress it and authentic self in glorious self-awareness.

Condemnation and chastisement given to you from outside based in the limited vision of others. You should not accept that. In many ways, acceptance requires cutting down the thorns of the brambles that life built around your heart and seeing self in your purest, most divine state of connection. That is acceptance. Cut down the brambles. Crawl out of the hole. Expose light of self to pure air. Thrive, knowing the paradox of condemnation and acceptance can be tilted in favor of light in the divine realization of self, of breath, of choice. As you sit here in the chair, fully human, the paradox exists in you as you breathe right now.

Acceptance lies in seeing truth exposed in light. Yourself, as is. Life, as is. Other humans, as is. Bifurcated paradox, yet one. Simple and complex. Spirit in human. Grasp it all. It is you. It is all.

Stop struggling with the comprehension of this. Acceptance requires letting go of struggle to see. All that is pain was given to you, suggested to you, imposed on you by people and events with their own limits and pain. You embrace it to the degree you invite it into yourself. It shapes as you allow. You dig the hole to incorporate this dark view to cloud your own light sense of spirit. You shift on the continuum to accommodate shade from the tree.

Your own self-awareness narrows as your spirit is defined from the outside in, from dark places in dark, safe holes.

And yet you are still there, existing side-by-side imbued with your truly divine light. Spirit challenge; see yourself as true self and not as damaged human.

Do not let someone or something else write your definition of self. You own your soul. It is up to you to define.

Live, breathe and as such your search is the inquiry into self. Who gets to decide how you live and breathe? Whether you cede that to outside or claim it for yourself? You do! Both options in your hands.

Who are you, really?

True self in spirit or story edited by the words and actions of those with troubles of their own? Up to you to find your rightful space on the continuum and live it. Breathe it.

Peace.

Aerial View
Reading 13

Trudge forward toward light and dispel the dark with true spirit light.

Take an aerial view of life and people.

Seek to 'see', develop insight from many angles into all that lives. Not just both sides, all sides.

Is un/happiness chronic or temporal, and can it be tempered to a semblance of happiness through compromise? Is aging un/kind, or a balance of changes good and bad? Yes and no. Always both. Many facets to consider. Answer usually yes…but…and…so. All correct, opposites existing side by side. Must see both sides. All sides. It is an act of love to consider all sides.

Does this denote understanding, and thus acceptance that requires honoring all facets of multifaceted situations and people?

If people are on the continuum of light and dark, can we adopt this view of these people and events?

A full-spectrum view.

And yet we cannot offer total acceptance of views that damage and inflict pain on others. While there can be recognition in a full-spectrum view, there is no reconciliation of their damaging nature to your acceptance of full view understanding.

Do dark forces belong in the valley of acceptance? Can their harmful nature be part of acceptance in the matrix when looking at the world of light and dark, or does dark deserve condemnation for negative energy/harm they contribute to the world?

The world yearns toward light and souls will fight for it because it is our moral imperative to create love and positive energy in the world.

Thus, all parts of the continuum are not equal in value. Accept that. Dark, negative energy is the work of harm on the continuum and needs light shone on it to dispel. If they refuse to see their own damaged child huddled in the dark, that does not mean the world has to dwell with them.

The onus is to fight for light, to illuminate all dark corners, to shed light on all energy connections and work to nurture and value those—to others, to life, to earth, to world, to universe, to the divine.

What do you owe the world of light and dark continuum? Light, of course, of refusal to allow dark to fracture soul's connections to the divine. Light is repair work—armaments in the struggle of the paradox.

Yes, some things are right and 'deserve' (limited human word) proactive engagement to minimize damage of dark.

Light warriors!

Shed light to understand the continuum, yes. Broaden your understanding of the matrix. See the paradox, but do not think that we are done here. Insight allows you to see pockets dark and use the power of your breath, your life, your now to enlighten.

Divine is all light. Those carrying dark torches, claiming to be for light are marching in the wrong direction, victims of their own dark natures. Use your bodies to shed light and extinguish the torches of dark.

That is your call to the divine. You can understand and accept dark as facet of continuum—but refuse to allow it equivalence. It is the responsibility of all to trudge forward toward light and dispel the dark with true spirit light.

Acceptance is not equivalence. It is recognition and understanding only. It lights our way to what we have to do and what we are up against to spread light into the world.

Diamond Heart
Reading 14

The diamond comes from fire, survives the fire, glows with fire.

Welcome to you. Thanks for opening today, a wonderful day of great message. Oh, how you are tangling within the tangle, searching for answers so far elusive.

Nature of the beast—

You will always struggle with knowing, almost knowing, not knowing—seeing, but not quite. That is it. Right there. Humanity/soul conundrum.

Clear knowing fogged over. Foggy knowing made clear. What to do with that?

That is full-spectrum seeing—not just seeing from all sides but seeing with full view of entanglements. The unclear is what you may see, so your efforts to chop down the brush, clear the blockage from your sight is your work, but so is the acceptance of the blocked, almost-view of life as human.

Shed as much light as you can on darkness. Examine the facets one and all. Hold them in your hands, but when you look and it remains unclear, that is it. You cannot know now. Maybe you will in a bit. Maybe never.

So, all those incessant questions and the disquiet they cause... embrace them, but not to worry—not problems.

Are you a problem? Do you have problems? Are you the problem? Do you have a problem seeing? Can you fix your problems? Do you cause your problems? Are people causing you problems?

Perhaps that is key to full-spectrum sight. When we begin to examine, attempt to see, we are constantly judging. That is a given, human endeavor, not a soul activity. We are really listening to earthly voices to define us/our joys/ our problems/ our lives—but full examination reveals much of the dialogue in our head is a production of the human mind, life, circumstance.

We are born in spirit, pure spirit in infant body and let the judgment begin! Good sleeper? Eater? Problem child? Good sibling, child, student, friend, spouse, worker, person?

All experiences result in filters that add color to the spectrum blocking some views, illuminating others. It colors each moment of your performance in circumstance. Really, to see clearly is to work to remove installed filters to see who you came here to be, how you shine and adapt to filters as part of life's challenges.

The tangle is your life experiences, the words others bestowed on you, the distortion of the purity, the hewing of the pure through trial and fire and glossing over, creating defenses.

Snip away the vines that block your thinking. Spritz away the fog that blocks your vision. Seek to see you in the purest form knowable in human form—the unadulterated, beautiful you undisturbed by the winds that buffet you.

Your real questions should be about the words, the messages, the earthly storm that swirled around you and caused you to retreat into the dark hole to protect yourself from flying debris. And yet, there you are. Fully formed and divinely connected. If made in God's image, how is it possible you are so flawed—a problem to be fixed?

Full-spectrum exposes all that is earthly you and glimpses of spirit you and reconciles your beauty amid the tangle. Both can exist, right? You can be at peace with the paradox. It is really that earthly and divine need to reconcile—both deserving of embrace.

Self, reconciled with self, tangled—yet purely perfect. Damaged, yet healed and whole.

See it all. Not for its contradiction, but for its truth.

The diamond comes from fire, survives the fire, glows with fire.

You, too. Truly you live unscathed in the heat of the tangle, at the heart of the tangle.

The problem is not the both. The "problem" is only embracing both in all moments, in all ways.

You are the diamond heart—fear not the brambles. They are yours, too.

Cosmic One
Reading 15

Is it love?

Welcome.

It is a holy time filled with connection to creator/energy of power/source of all life. Need to see that is all day—all days—not just this time of year. Connections are everywhere; to each other, to the divine.

This 'holiday' celebration very human connection that is a good reminder. But every day is a divine gift with an opportunity to connect.

Humans are so limited but designed that way as a study in contrasts in order to grow in search for truth of existence, of connection, of degrees of insight and steps in growth.

Relax and take it all in with confident acceptance.

Humans are what they are—flawed in body, limited in experience, divine energy constrained—destined to struggle, but to feel range of emotions in ways that free spirit energy cannot.

Accept that, too. There is a dichotomy of human/spirit connection, flawed yet perfect, united in same struggle to attain insight. Some are further along than others. Slow down to see it. Feel it. Appreciate it.

It is. You are. Two forms as one, with focus on one. Others, too.

So that balance plays out in every day with humans flailing, spirit glowing—always tilting one way or the other seeking balance of guaranteed love of self, of others, of divine.

Human form is so limited, so misguided at times, yet capable of such, well, humanity—a component necessary for spirit development.

So as others around you 'celebrate' their human connection to the divine in religious, human ways, accept the limits presented by human. Accept, but do not condone, misguided behavior that preys on the worst of human limitations.

You can believe and recognize it is there, but always allow your divine/positive human to spring forth in defense of good. Protect those who cannot defend themselves while here. They are an earthly test, an opportunity for spirit growth which is really strengthening ties to the divine.

Tend to your own garden of growth, but part of that entails, no requires, you to be a defender of good in the world. Simply one question will help you discern this.

Is it love?

Love is your divine connection, your glow of existence, your purpose, your growth.

Is it love?

Simple question—struggle with answer really not all that hard. Loving path usually clearer, easier to see acts of love—feeding, supporting, sharing, giving—not so hidden and not so hard. Individual choice to not only live, but defend, eternal light not through war, hate, deprivation, condemnation.

But through acceptance, followed by expression of loving spirit energy—your responsibility. Use power to grow your own love connections to the divine, but also to express that as body lives out its term.

You are defending spirit and love when you do, so try to do it with spirit, not condemnation of human in mind. How you use your human spirit energy and earthly opportunities are the ultimate in acceptance. You can only do what you can do—but you are called by good to enact it.

But loving spirit means looking, embracing, acting in ways that view human and spirit as one in totality, not two separate facets.

It is all one diamond, far from flawless, and your heart serves as center for carrying out divine spirit calling in earthly body. It is the beacon to guide you through the darkness, dissolve the barriers between the two and see insight as the lantern within that governs this time and all time—centered in the divine heart connection to human actions to spirit—that binds them all. A triad that is one star and flows throughout time, space—all.

All. One = all. You are a piece of it.

In the broader landscape lens, see all in others, in ourselves, in divine panorama. Much of our lesson exists in plain view. During 'holidays' humans present themselves with an opportunity to see grand plan that exists in all times.

Pause. Take a deep breath. Put your human fingers on the lens of the cosmic camera and fiddle with the lens to see what you can see of the vast scope that is your existence. Then sit quietly if it comes into view.

Look. Feel. Embrace.

Love.

It really embodies the cosmic one.

Divine Revelations
Reading 16

Learning to feel love is a loving act, not a thinking act.

Revelations.

To welcome spirit is to open heart, to enrich vision, to live at peace with self as is. If you think spirit ever calls for you to shut a door in your heart towards someone different or something fearful, it is not spirit. It is human side seeking protection from hurt.

Spirit installs windows, then dissolves them completely so your energy can heal and flow and live in love. You will be able to see self as is and love the flawed visage—and see connections to all 'flawed' around you—perfect in spirit, damaged in ego.

See to use your own new vision to live in spirit—heart wide open to spread love. It is your calling to live as loving, loved self in world badly in need of it. Opening your heart allows you to 'see' from all angles, a fuller view of all healed/unhealed, flawed and flawless. Excited, yet blunted out of fear, struggling for the thing you need most and to protect from pain inflicted. Side by side. One pain/joy can be accepted with pure sight and insight—through heart wide open.

You will protect yourself. Your heart will see all and allow safe vision of love that defines us. We yearn for it.

If you keep spirit heart flowing, your revelations will enhance your love, nurture love. Love yourself. Love others. Spirit window links soul with outside and serves as conduit within and provides deeper connections to beyond—the beyond you on earth and the beyond you in spirit.

Envision yourself as spark, a light in a vast array of lights. Safely glowing in dark surround, sparking energy bursts of joy, feeling own heat of energy, connecting to complex network of universal energy that is shared in love.

The biggest revelation of all? You have an untapped well of love that connects deep into yourself, the divine and all others.

It is always there.

Revelations are love in action of connection. See it. Touch it. Let it touch you as a conduit of your human time in joyous, divine revelations that are loving. Live it out in daily actions, a weapon against darkness and hate.

Revelation is heart wide open turned into insight played out in action. Embraced. Connected. Illuminated. Grace is a gift of divine bestowed on you in divine heart connection to live joyously in divine, loving action.

Let the well flow. Gaze out the window. Look in and out.

Feel the rush of joy in revelations, not just of divine love for you, but the divine connection linking you to all others.

Cosmic opening of eyes, heart, self, connection. Too vast for humans to grasp in totality. Too painful not to try.

See vast and small. Embrace vast and small. Connect to vast and small. Love vast and small. Praise that is revealed to you. See, understand, embrace, love.

Revelations—love alive!

Surprising, unplanned. Break down the expected, the restrictive patterns, thoughts, requirements that impede revelation. What in human blocks seeing? These walls do not protect you. Loving acceptance protects you as it opens to the power of the divine and diminishes fear of the human.

Challenge for you—let it flow. It all flows.

Thinking can be building blocks of walls. This is a message for you—

Revelation comes when walls are removed, thinking is limited. Learning to feel love is a loving act, not a thinking act.

Revelation not an act of thinking, it is an act of flow. You just tried to think through this message and you felt it stop, because here is your lesson—revelation only comes when your heart is in charge and your mind takes a rest from its inexorable desire to control.

Revelation is paradox to control. Ironic? Make conscious decision—control your need for control and love will flourish. Oh, the irony of life!

You find what you seek only after you stop carefully planning the search; stop installing all the necessaries for a safe expedition.

Happy travels! Unplanned and dangerous. Best revelatory opportunities occur if you stay open hearted to seeing and banish the rituals, plans, traditions that restrict you.

Loving Indulgence
Reading 17

Kindly indulge your folly and wave as it passes by.

First reading of the year, but you do realize that word 'year' is not real. It is a human construct, but humans do like to define parameters, so it serves you as a member of earthly community to celebrate yearly 'fresh' start.

See, however, swirling continuation flowing of past, this moment and that to come—again, this moment is all that exists for you, so if you want it to be 'new', so be it!

That is your charge as human—indulgence.

As you realize the vast scope of connected existence, and your little pinprick of light, you can become more accepting of all that this means. You are human. You are spirit. You are a piece of larger energy. Paradoxes abound with perfection/imperfection being today's focus. Neither is really a valid term. Perfect means nothing. Imperfect not its opposite.

Is—only thing.

The perfect/imperfect merely human attempt to explain life force progression, sitting in judgment. That is all that is. Accepting the perfect, admonishing and refuting the imperfect.

Silly. It all just is.

Knowing that means you can really indulge yourself in love and experience always. You are. In all facets. The hurt, pride, joy, kindness, love, hate, the best of you, the worst of you—in your opinion.

Judge life force only on how you conduct yourself as steward of your universal place and divine connection. Seek not to harm anyone, anything in the matrix, but seek to indulge yourself as integral energy that lives, breathes, learns. Here are words to your detriment: best/worse, good/bad, loved/unloved, flawed/perfect.

Close your eyes and embrace the swirling energy of yours made up of is—how in this moment you can be all these opposites at once, with no contradiction. In fact, there is no contradiction. It is you. You are. All this human and spirit and divine can be one even if it is not consistent in your human eye.

What you are right now is all. So why not accept? Why not indulge? Learn about the breadth and scope of you and caress it all. Without human words. You who lives by words and uses words to comprehend should try to erase them and see without them. Feel without labels. Understand without processing to write a narrative.

You can see it. Now, can you live that? Recognize judgment when you see it. Let it sweep over you and by you and past you into the vapor. It is not you.

Kindly indulge your folly and wave as it passes by—yes, it is part of you, but no, it isn't you.

Waves of human attempt to control, repel, analyze true spirit. Isn't that funny? Can't you see the humor? Can you embrace the feelings, indulge the feelings, then send them on their way before the energy you expend to maintain them engulfs you in darkness? Release, erase, embrace, allow—free.

It is all part of you, but not you. You envision yourself as multi-faceted structure of energy, distinct in the field of energy and these waves come from you, propel you, guide you—darken you, but they do not have to.

A knowing nod, then let them go! Soon you will see those delineating walls dissolve and you will see yourself more as one. But not yet. Work on releasing the words you use to define self, your experience.

Yes, there you are. No difference/line between spirit and human.

Stop living your life by drawing lines with words and images that fuel your limitations.

Dissolving, erasing, building, glowing, accepting, indulging, swirling energy of your spirit currently living in body. You will be surprised to find how you live out of body.

Can you imagine? In spirit/in body human, same connection here. Out of body, can it be so different?

You are.

Accept that moment of breath means just that. Nothing more here or there.

You are given what you need to know when you can know it.

Soul Etchings
Reading 18

It etches a story on your soul existence for you alone.

Use your hands to tell the story beyond the eyes.

Oh, the energy flows in the cold as well as the heat. Watch the universe play out in all its glory—hot/cold, safe/dangerous, large/small, human/spirit.

And then move smaller and realize large and small exist on all those levels. Large in small. Small in large. Your place in matrix can be all these—as is the matrix energy field.

Okay, where does that put us? Center of all large and small with many facets.

Your vision is a multisided sphere, floating in a vast universe of dark and light. Watch it all melt. The sphere, walls of sphere are the brain trying to 'see' beyond comprehension. Watch it all melt into one.

Your life right now is one with all other sparks of energy in all times. Some that existed 'then', those that exist 'now' and those that will exist. Even that idea of time human construct—the idea that all things are divided into three time zones of past, present and future. Just like time zones and time and lines on a map—all human construct. Your soul life separation is a construct, too.

We are getting at something bigger. Now—and it is multilayered and vast. Maybe it becomes a mark on the energy to record what happened, maybe not. For what purpose? The mark is made on your soul life, though, as you live it out in many incarnations. So small as human, yet so overwhelming in its feeling capacity.

Think beyond just energy as existence. Think of it as in motion, action. Your energy is currently in body to take that form of action, but its record is soul etched and imprint is part of you as record. You have done this to detail eons that stretch before and stretch back.

Let's go back to the book of life. "Books" just soul etching of you and your intersections with all as you blaze an infinite push toward light.

Reexamine, then, the large impact of despair as light quencher and take soul etchings into your own hands for this short blip on the screen.

You are given the gift of larger insight, broader perspective. You came doubting words and dictates of others, which allows you to be free of dissuasion, to see larger scope without human veil. Although you have veil as human, you were given enough distance to pull curtain back and embrace without rules told by others.

Your authentic self is allowed to see source of problem self for your adaptation to circumstances and questioning of details. Value that in self. Seek to embrace as much infinite light that a human can embrace. True self sees beyond, around, though, in, between, on, over . . . all means of interconnection.

Continue that struggle as it etches a story on your soul existence for you alone. All others must search for themselves, so honor that.

Your search is not theirs. Your knowing is not theirs. Your insight remains with you—your contribution to the one within and beyond.

Purpose is clear vision for self—perhaps messages for others. Maybe not. Each soul journey both connected and alone.

Minute. Infinite. See that in all—in spectrum of knowing dictated by our own willingness to see, our own courage to seek and to know.

Take the tumbling sphere and dissolve it. Dissolve the words, the lines, the images, the emotions, the human, the spirit, the large and the small.

Know in other ways and soul etchings will enlighten you beyond your wildest imaginings.

Vast longing to know brings enlightenment for those willing to embrace the infinite.

Stop there. Do not pause to process with your words. The soul is speaking to you. Stop right this second and listen.

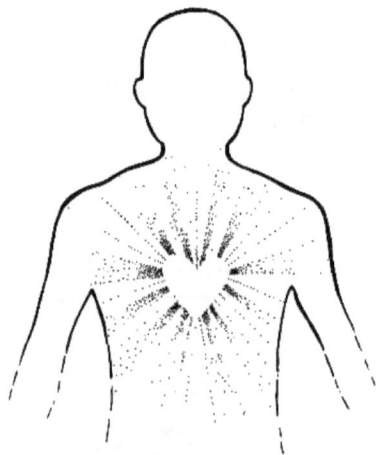

Flawed Perfection

Reading 19

It is all how it is meant to be.

Dearest one. Happy connection! A topic which plagues you on this day.

What are the strings that connect? Can humans develop soul strings or are the ties on earth something else? Let's just say yes. A blanket of energy supports you in the matrix. Bright, strong lines of energy may connect you to others. Maybe not.

In humans, emotions grow these ties, although it is hard to discern true connection. So many people believe connection that does not exist and ignore connections that do. All fits with the dim view of human eyes—so much darkness shrouding soul.

BUT.
That is how it is supposed to be.
It is all how it is supposed to be.

I can hear you from here—why? The human/soul's deepest question—the one with a million answers, yet none at all.

The connections you seek there primarily human, but you are looking for soul connection instead, thus the disconnect you feel, floating in the abyss alone—longing for something that is not commonly supposed to be.

Busy little bees flying about pollinating the flowers, creating sweetness. Living stinging lives, short lived, unaware of bigger picture, driven to do something they do not understand that is minutely vital. That is life on all levels.

They do not have the emotions of humans, but how are we to know how it feels for them in the matrix? Whether we understand or not does not matter.

In fact. It is all as it is meant to be.

Stop there. Feel that. Know it heartily—of heart, in heart.

Certainly, they can move the hive, sting if annoyed, work collectively or not. In all—meant to be—even change. Adaptation meant to be.

Now adapt your view of it to know how life thrives—humans/bees all working toward divine sweetness, but oh-so-not a divinely straight path.

It is all how it is meant to be.

The plagues of your life all part of fabric of energy. Do not struggle to shake off the bonds of human frailty. Those blinders are inherent in our experience—as is enlightenment for those seeking to peer beyond the hive.

If you do not understand one—or the other—it is all how it was meant to be.

That does not mean life's chronology predetermined. It means life in its grand scale takes place beyond knowing all. It plays out as designed. Darkness and light. All energy, all around, all bigger than us and microscopic in orchestration. You cannot know everything and yet you cannot stop trying to, so carry on knowing it is all truly significant, bathed in energy grand, free flowing, sparking and connected—and not.

You can know your corner, you can glimpse the vast. But what is in between is life lived—so much harder to understand in its complex contradictions.

Sit with this. Your deepest part knows the soul as both the divine unknown within, and the vast unknown beyond.

Your life lived struggles to connect the two—as it was intended to. It is all what it is supposed to be.

Bask in those waves for a moment—
Even the confusion makes sense—

Like the human body—complex—or a simple machine we can 'fix' when it is broken but cannot save when it is done. Where in it lies the soul? The self? The heart pulsing beyond the beating pump?

Life and energy are like that. So much we know, so much we try by strength of will to master and so much we will never know or master no matter how we toil because it is beyond us to see it here. Flawed, yet perfect: you, life, energy, divine, connection, matrix, knowing, self, others, soul, humanity.

Flawed perfection.

Dwell there in truth.

Bigger Visions
Reading 20

The most human decision of all is what you choose to see.

Greetings from afar—or so near—or both.

The cycle of time unfolds before you in a tableau of endeavor, played out on so many levels. Human spirit, life force pulsing in body and beyond.

So, how does that play out in bigger scope? Like a piano, this pen, all human tools . . . we grasp them for activity, believe we are in control of the outcome—that the piano is silent if we are not playing it. But sitting on the piano bench, know the piano may be silent, but the world outside that silence continues to pulse. The energy outside of and beyond human continues to flow. Thus is the locus of your control if you continue to focus on the piano and insist it is only proof of life. You, after all, control this pen, your piano.

But in harboring such a view, you miss indescribable chords of celestial music—vision beyond the keys because the most human decision of all is what you choose to see. Your daily choices of sight endless. How do you see self? Others? Fellow earthly beings beyond you? Animals? Trees? Life? The divine? That which is beyond all human comprehension?

So many levels. So many windows. We stand before them every day and we choose which ones to look out of, peer into, or close.

Try to envision the vast array of insight choices that await you in the hall of glass. Know that each vision presents itself closed, skewed or true. People close the blinds to the scenes they want to ignore. They redesign the scenes that do not suit them—but they rarely sit back and ponder what lies before them in truth which is presented to them in pathways suited to their attributes. So human of us to fail to see the vastness. So human of us to see the scene we wish to see, failing to even suspect the rearrangement into truth as you wish it to be.

What to do when faced with such an array of truths filtered through human lens?

Truth—such an elusive idea! Your truths. The truths. Hard to tell through hooded eyes.

Therein lies the truth.

You will never see it and yet you have to try.

Expand your sight beyond the piano before you. Look around you at all the windows that await exploration. Then dissolve the windows to see something greater beyond that construct and see life divine pulsing around you, all connected.

Then, how could you hate? Destroy? Plunder? Exploit? Fear? Diminish?

What you do to energy reverberates throughout the matrix and pushes back at you. See beyond the words that shape our thoughts, the images that clench in our minds. Find the metaphor that helps explain, but then dissolve that into energy to see what lies beyond the human. Construct to aid understanding the walls that divide, the windows that shield, the emotions that produce voices that protect.

Goal must be to live wide open to what lies beyond, untouched by human hands, unshaped by human experience.

Know you will only grasp a tiny corner of fabric, but it will tether you to greater truth and insight and peace and love. Recognize it has its shading of dark uncertainties. All that exists here exists there but know that connection is the path to the divine—inspired and energized by connected acts of love enacted here while in body.

Live life pondering the keys of the piano but be aware that all your power swirls around you in areas of seeing beyond that experience.

It will serve you well, however, to step aside from what you think is the only activity that you deem important. Raise your eyes. Scan the room beyond the walls. Look for the light filtering through the windows. Part the curtains if you dare.

When you open your eyes as one newly unblind, be sure your eyes are as fresh and untainted as possible, knowing the truth is not carved in stone. It pulses with energy and that energy infuses us all with light divine.

See the truth in the mountains unmoving and the shifting sea and the frenetic movement of earthly life and the vast universe beyond.

Bigger visions expand the mind, heart, soul—divine to see.

Put the period there.

Experiential Truths
Reading 21

Create the ripples. Where they emanate is beyond your control.

Greetings from here and there. Peace and grace are what you seek and asking questions about those questions produces questions that raise more questions. Can you see the disquiet in that?

A question is an acknowledged gap in knowing—seeking the constant answer to life's uncertainty. The irony, of course, is that such seeking creates a persistent lack of knowing. It produces a churn of unease. If only you could find the answer.

A life full of seeking and never finding—the constant state of almost knowing—produces unrest, dissatisfaction due to the chase of the elusive. Might you consider knowing—now?

You know what you know. Now. Constantly asking questions places your happiness of now on hold and projects your satisfaction as tentative in the future, dependent on finding that answer at another point on the continuum.

We have already discussed the fact that 'the future' is a figment of hopeful imaginations. We hope to control it, influence it, shape it to fit our deepest yearnings, and yet it doesn't really exist. It never has and it never will.

The past exists in story. The now exists in experience. The future? Nothing, really. So, while we think what we are doing now give us an element of control over what WILL happen, in reality living now only gives us a semblance of influence over living—now. The story will be written through a lens and what happens now is done as soon as it happens.

There are too many factors at play in the world to believe that saving pennies now will result in a future due to your influence. Place your bets, really. What will happen, will happen. Those pennies may make your life better later. Maybe not. All bets are off. Why do we keep placing our bets? Gambling on the future?

Humans often farm out the now to the past (as extremely influential) or the future (as inordinately important) to detract from the uncertainty of now, our choices in the moment. If I had a terrible past due to _____, then I can spend my now asking questions and devoting my life to a happier future. Place your bets.

The cornerstone of now is what to do with it? Hah! A reading about questions that asks a question! Life is experience. Experience is now. The answer to all questions is how you choose to live now.

Perhaps a shift in our timeline is necessary. Let questions arise and reside IN THE PAST. This happened. The question arises, how did this influence me? Now here is the key shift. The answer is your action in this moment here and now. The answer does not lie in a life devoted to generating questions that may lead to an answer of a happy future. See?

Current thought—now is mired in uncertainty, the future a gamble at best. As soon as you ask any question it drifts into the past and you place your heart into future hopes for an answer. When is it time to live your lessons learned? When do you shift focus from questions to answers?

Your life choices answer those questions. Fleeting answers are shaped by so many forces within and without. Shifting from now moment to life matrix energy story is a flicker. Now exists at all times. What good is a question without an answer?

Such as "Will I ever be happy?" Can you see the problem with asking that in this moment? Your past story records you were not happy. You are asking if that will change in the future. That cycle will never produce a happy moment for you. The correct 'answer' is not even a question. It is a decision. Choosing happiness in this very moment, at this very time. Mind boggling. Such a shift since waking up full of questions. Will I be happy today (?) and then waiting for your cards to fall on the table, the roulette ball to fall into the right hole, waiting for yes to become clearer before bedtime.

Declarative statement—I will live today happily.

Can you see how the day may progress differently? Exhausting, really, to own this all the time. It is so much easier to place it into the hands we have known, or the hands we have yet to see.

Our own hands—in this moment—that is where declarative truths belong. Here you go, asking all those questions again. But what about blame? How will this change my life? Can I do this? It is right? Open your hands. They are empty at the moment, but they are your instruments of experiential truth, powerfully wrought by you in each breath and action. It is an overwhelming responsibility, true, yet an unavoidable truth which is given to you to see.

Shift the timeline. Allow your past questions to shape your current reality. Sit in the moment and feel the real value of now wash over you and redefine what will 'make you happy' in the future.

Claim it now as the only true reality. The only power that you own. It exists in the most mundane and the most exciting, the satisfying and the terrifying.

We shall not record all those questions that keep knocking at the door. Right here. It is fine. It is not yours to rewrite the past or fix the broken world. Live the best moment you can in every moment you are given. It is the only power you have been given.

Legacy is merely the retelling of the way you chose to live your moments.

You are thinking too much about this. Already this is past. See how fleeting?

Who knows the future importance of this experience? Live now. Create the ripples.

Where they emanate is beyond your control.

Right. Now.

Let it go, let it flow.

Greetings dear one.

Of interest to you—life! All around in damaged bodies and pure spirits. All perfect in the ways of creation and existence.

So, can you accept all the truth in opposites? Expand your mind beyond the pain and brokenness to the perfection in all life—playing out in celestial chords of harmony far beyond the screeching of the bow and the clinking missteps of the piano player.

Trite can dwell in truth and truth can dwell in contradiction and you dwell in the heart of energy while residing alone outside of boundaries. Connection it is—again—the vitality and variance of it is expansive.

As you envision the life fire pulsing, connecting, know those lights flashing link to you. Link to all.

Everyone's veins of light connection are unique in time and place—always there/sometimes masked, sometimes darkened. Snipped, sewn, loosened, tightened, depending on time, places, soul choices.

Can we get to acceptance on that? If indeed true, you ask, then why the longing for what you have, but do not?

Those threads glow at the soul level. The support of the divine, the network of connection to others very stalwart, a given beyond and behind the curtain that divides spirit and human. Heavy, weighted beyond your comprehension on terra firma. You would live so differently if only you knew.

Exactly the point.

You are in body and one spirit decision is to whom you link. Which chords to illuminate and maintain and which chords to lie fallow, like fields to be brought back to life with water of love divine.

Humans are broken, masked to a degree, hobbled by body limited, emotions sensitive, intellect malleable and experiences imperfect.

Imperfect such a flawed word to encapsulate that. It is all perfectly designed for growth as neither spirit life nor human life is able to grasp everything that resides in both realms.

Fiery twins are human and spirit, linked by deep heart ties and desire to grow towards the divine. Ignorant of one another, desperate for one another, yearning to unite, but so unable to do so—a stumbling dance of love perfect in its graceful progress toward knowing, uniting.

There you are—an answer for the ages—but can you embrace it? Live it courageously! Know the pain and wonder of human, sacred in its perfect imperfection. Life in spirit desires to feel richness and frailty and reckless courage and foolish heart with genuine love on two levels. See two as one beyond the idea that something is missing, failing.

No, it is not.

In totality, it is real. It is always us. All the time. Who says pain is bad? "Failure" should be avoidable? Human is a plague to overcome?

Life in spirit and human is just one big classroom brimming with the power of experience to transform—so, abandon the fallacy the future will be better if I can overcome my human frailty. So many things wrong with that idea.

In humanness, do not believe the future lies in your hands; that you as almighty are responsible for and guilty of the frailties of pain, disconnect inherent in human. Ah, watch the human join hands with the spirit and waltz around the room (bumping into all those obstacles)—now.

Do so—not to create a better future, but to create a rich and full tolerance for all facets of the diamond. Ouch! That is pain. Wow! That is joy. Can be both at once in the dance of life supreme.

Seek to find the heart cord that links you to spirt and all others beyond and the divine. Flip the switch to let the energy flow. Applaud as it grows and when it stumbles.

Welcome it as you. Call you by your name. Embrace your dual nature and caress the wounds and the beauty and the unity.

Let it go, let it flow. When they intersect, the spark of the divine illuminates now at the core of a heart-lived life.

The NOW portal lives and provides a keyhole between human and spirit. There is peace in peering through, only to see yourself peering back. A hug—and a wink—and well wishes; all yours for the seeing.

All is right. Now.

All is. Right now.

Treasure Hunt
Reading 23

The challenge of human experience is to find the soul's voice.

Welcome to a mere moment in time—a snapshot in living—taken at any moment. That is what you create. This moment and nothing more. AKA life!

Creation spawns creation, but who knows where those snapshots will take you? You mistakenly believe that if you stage this image to be captured in this moment, in this way, future images may result in what you want to happen. If you could only look this way now, the future will look _____.

Best not to worry about that. This snapshot captures life as lived now, not how life will be lived. Maybe. If you decide to take the snapshot in Italy, do not rest on the assurance that later photos of you will show you speaking Italian, laughing with Italian friends or basking in the Tuscan sun. Point being—don't invest too much in images that have not been taken.

Now. Now. Now. Now. Now—cannot stress that enough. Spending time creating in mind's eye scenes that you wish would happen is a twofold mistake. It squanders now by placing it on hold and it is futile to expend energy trying to create something you cannot. It is wasted time and effort, really.

Let's discuss time as currency. It is the only thing you have, for whatever span you have it. Like currency you spend it. Oh, the hand wringing that surrounds that expenditure! Questions, questions, questions that ironically impede your life. Am I using it wisely? Is it a life well spent? Or wasted?

How can I plan (future tense) to use it better? Lists? Resolutions?

Whew! Exhausting, really. How about you just live? Not mindlessly—during which you fail to appreciate life's beauty. And not mindfully, where you fret about instilling value in each moment as the best possible, the deliberate choice you made in the past to carefully construct the present. So fraught with pressure and anxiety! What if I am NOT mindful? Am I being wasteful if I just breathe in the air of this everyday moment without noting—or creating fireworks to enhance its beauty?

Oh, the pressure of having too much time to (mindfully) contemplate time! What a cosmic joke, of which there are many.

Think about how people can feel so intensely, so badly about something that just is! Worry. Fret. Worry. Plan. Bemoan. Suffer. Correct. Control.

Time is. Love is. Emotion is. You are. Right now. Regardless of what you are 'doing.' Living is not a ledger.

Have you done it right? Did you praise your children correctly? How are you at your job? Marriage? If you can just accept you are, and live life with love daily, that is that. Simple.

Live to live, infusing heart into daily acts. That is it. Where is the despair in that? How can you fret over that? This is not weight! Time is not judgment!

Past snapshots exist as moments in time where you lived a certain way, to some degree orchestrated in a dance of self and others. You can construct the scrapbook of images but beware the effect of paralyzing now with despair of past or anxiety of future.

Take a snapshot right now. Look at what you are doing. We have encouraged you to minimize questions in the moment, but this warrants examination. What is causing this? What earthly concerns are building roadblocks of censorship to this message? What can't you accept about this?

You are letting unheard voices from the past enter the narrative. Their voices will always be with you as past accumulation but living in now requires you to give them voice, but not influence.

Which voice is narrating the now? Who is speaking, framing the image, directing the camera at the moment? Who gets to drive the car and who gets to ride shotgun and who are the backseat drivers and who is locked in the trunk when the flash goes off? Essential understanding of now, right? Who gets the solo in the choir now?

Try to hear the voices with more discernment. Your authentic soul-self sings with the choir but is often silenced by the louder voices of human experience because they have been on earth with you recently, so their painful volume is turned up. Spirit self lies quietly, waiting, often behind the curtain that separates earth from the spirit realm, but it is there.

The challenge of human experience is to find the soul's voice. Listen to its wisdom. Turn up its volume. It is the voice of love and connection and should be the driver of now—the loving parent to embrace all others and let the journey proceed in peace.

Let that roil for a bit, yes? Remember. Circle back. Who are you, really?

The answer to that question does not await you in the future. It is in you now. You are now.

Such a treasure hunt! The beauty that lies in this moment! Unearthing true you—a treasure chest of love and delight. What each snapshot of now should record.

You living in the moment as soul in body.

Thankfully. Safely. Happily.

Day 1
Reading 24

Gently learn your own truth.

Gray day. Only what you can see. Above the clouds a brilliant blue. Hear little chirps of hope in rainy days.

What does that mean to you and all others?

Life teems on—gray here, blue there, hopeful chirps, loud thunder and flashing lightning followed by peaceful moments of quiet.

You are always saying hurry up! Hurry up! Get to the message. Good luck with that on all levels.

Sit in one place. Gaze around. Listen. Check into the pulse. Understand the blue. Alone. Here you are. Stripped of all connection, concern.

Who are you, sitting there within this life? Really?

Now that you have met and known your earthly self through responsive voices, let your authentic self walk out into the open. Raise her hand in connection with all other facets of self. Hand open to others, held aloft. Arms wide open, staying in the flow of the energy.

Announcing, *"I am here. This is mine. I've got this. Thank you so much for keeping me safe, but I will have to give this a try. I know your number. I recognize your voice. I will call if I need help. But for now, I'd like to give it a go, carry the weight, see what I am made of and let myself meet myself for the very first time."*

Soak it in. Get to know the whole of you. What does she like? Hate? Love? Embrace? What makes her happy? Fulfilled? Embraced by being in the right space basking in the right energy?

Release all those things you couldn't. Wouldn't. See? Embracing story of self to set you free—first, to discover the story you wrote and then to create the story you are.

Pen in hand you took life experiences and transcribed them—all the responsive voices recorded in your stead. Such an earthly story. Book in hand, network of energy created by human truth, through human eyes, felt by human heart.

Once a discovery of what you COULD do, now we can see who you are.

All those voices—resilience, hurt, discouragement, determination—are really part of your fabric, but only the blanket that swaddles you. They will always be with you.

But the protective swaddle can be unbound and the cloak removed.

The journey of spirit is really a discovery of authentic self, a revelation of who you are—really—even when life unfolds in bumpy waves. And yet, there you are.

The narrative will be established, but the mystery yet unsolved because so much remains to be known.

What does the soul self really want? To know true self—to connect to energy through love, to develop in strides towards the divine.

Oh, so you knew that love was important, and it was related to acceptance, but you always felt your challenge was to love others. Could you do that?

No, because it was love at secondary level. Must love and accept true self first, embrace your own light first—perfectly flawed perfection eternal.

Go no further than that.

You have seen her emerge with hand outstretched asking, "Who am I, really?"

Yes, the cacophony of voices that are woven into your fabric are part of your identity, but they are not you. Stand there alone by the mirror. Look intently at who has emerged.

Question it all. Ask the questions. Get acquainted. You only owe it to yourself this time through to gently learn your own truth.

If you do, it will amaze you. Unite self with self. What comes of life after that? Remember, future not the goal here.

Right now is your call to self, care of self, love of self. It is a core strength that enables you to live now authentically, accepting of life broadly conceived. The cloak of gray day can lift to reveal the brilliance of love unshielded.

That is enough.
For now. For love.
For the love of now.
For the love of self.

Let the first day begin when you finally meet yourself.

Day 1.

Enough Said
Reading 25

Whereto goes the heart muffled in darkness?

You come here as one spirit in one body connected to universal energy—and then human occurs.

How you live it depends on how you respond to the events, the waves that wash over you.

From then on, the needle moves on the continuum of enlightenment. If human prevails, the emotions weave around spirit to protect it. Due to short sight, it might also block it.

Loving protection/protective blindness can create an imbalance—living a partial, inauthentic life steeped in unease and perhaps disquiet and perhaps unhappiness.

Whereto goes the heart muffled in darkness? Darkness can engulf without a release of soul authentic into light of universal energy.

There are many narrators of the story you are living now. Listen carefully to all, to those known and those 'safely' concealed.

To live fully the human cannot protect or negate the spirit. Both should live fully, proudly in bonds of loving devotion and respect.

Put this revelation front and center in now to embrace the whole of you—healed and loving in your own embrace.

See the light of that reflected in the divine mirror.

Enough for a life to learn. Rest there in peace.

Heart Song 3- Expand

Reading 1- Full Spectrum Experience
Reading 2- Boom. Hearts alive!
Reading 3- Story in Truth
Reading 4- Own This Moment
Reading 5- Today is Destination
Reading 6- Body and Spirit
Reading 7- Align Micro/Macro
Reading 8- Cleave One Breath
Reading 9- Perfect in Place
Reading 10- See the Wonder
Reading 11- Creation of Purpose
Reading 12- Opening Patient Eyes
Reading 13- Holes and Vistas
Reading 14- Eternal Light Force
Reading 15- Listening with Spirit
Reading 16- The Alchemist's Eyes
Reading 17- Embrace 360° Theater
Reading 18- Co-create Destiny
Reading 19- Power of Yet
Reading 20- 1,001 Layered Stories
Reading 21- Helpful and Hopeful
Reading 22- Arrogance and Judgment
Reading 23- Here's the Thing
Reading 24- The Magic Answer
Reading 25- Every Day Crossroads

Full Spectrum Experience
Reading 1

You are not alone.

Welcome to Heart Song 3!

Oh, you of preconceived notions, seeking answers. Best we can advise—

Listen.

Heart Song 2 was learning about self, finding, peering into authentic soul self, surrounded by narrators—a story of you at center—embraced by friends and protections of self that are designed to shield you from hurt. You have met them. Now what?

That was key to next phase of adventure.

We have given you bread crumbs. You are authentic self, unique to experience while in body and spirit. You struggled deep to find self, hiding in corner, hardened in heart protected by stone walls.

Now what?

Again, it is part of a message of unraveling the mystery, exposing the truth of you. Now how about doing the same for connection to others?

For you are not alone.

You have yourself at center, but rays of light flow two ways. You can look in, but you are also part of a vast network of energy connection. You do not know this yet.

So, we will explore self's connection to the world through pulsing energy—to this point unseen and unknown. A whole new set of revelations await you in the exploration, the key word of which is OUT. Think OUT.

In Heart Song 2, the key word was in—looking in as relative to all experiences human and spiritual. Now you are looking out—at the vast expanse of connection human and spirit, with the emphasis on same process—exploring, understanding, exposing, developing and ultimately, living, in broader connection of self (truly) to larger matrix of interactions.

Examine alone as part of human experience. Examine pain and joys of connection as part of comprehensive human/spirit-lived life incarnation.

You are both alone and connected—another paradox. For so long, the alone has been dominate. Now, perhaps it is time for that to be accepted and even embraced as part of the opposite ONE that resides in all truth.

Construction, yes, but more a journey of discovery and ultimately acceptance of that which is.

Yes, you are both alone and connected, now how can that truth become life in motion? A rich life full of understanding and appreciation of truth here and beyond.

How can this become soul satisfying, moving you closer to truth and the divine?

Perhaps the better thought is soul fulfillment, enlightenment, nurturing, knowing more, loving more, soul satisfying in infinite ways.

Growing ever more aware, ever stronger in the light.

Forge on in the movement toward living vividly alive in body and spirit.

Take these lessons and live richly in the moment, knowing you are perfect and accepting these terms for growth.

You are soul living alive! Continue the dance! Hear the music! Embrace self, life, positive, negative, emotions, pain, joy, connection and disconnection all as one.

You cannot have light without dark shadows to expose the nuanced beauty of the image.

No artist paints only in light. Their creativity flourishes through the use of light to illuminate and portray the beauty in the existence of full spectrum experiences.

You, too. All.

Artists in life divine.

Peace.

Boom. Hearts Alive!

Reading 2

Explore your energy with fanfare.

Seismic shifts can come as calming whispers.

Yes, you know it is different now. The kaleidoscope continues to swirl, shift, vibrate. But now dear, brilliant beauty reigns.

Your expectation of a clear, solid view is dispelled. Look at life through the kaleidoscope instead and relish the joy of all that it is—uncertain yet beautiful, with flecks of dark and flecks of joy.

And it is you. All you, and all us, and all energy, and all life in constant motion—beautiful, but transient; oh you, who desires concrete beneath your feet. That has not served you well for love or for growth.

The movement of the flecks so much more invigorating. There you are. Part of it.

Are you getting the point? Your life is your vision as you choose to construct it. It can indeed be the concrete as a bunker for you. Or it can be swirling bursts of color.

All things exist as all possibilities.

Construction by you, for you. Not by you for others, or by others for you. Reality is constructed as you wish to see it and live it. But beyond the vista you create is so much more just waiting for you to see it. Touch it. Create it.

Your existence is an act of creation. You who have always said, "I am not creative" chose to create that inaccurate reality.

Irony—you were creating your own lack of creativity—mind blowing! Heart exploding!

Envision taking all that you believe and pushing the lever on the bomb and watching all the flashy specks fly out in joyful recognition of creation.

But you are not blowing up the heart or your false reality. You are liberating yourself from all the blocks you created, the concrete you used to build the gray-walled compound.

So yes, spirit energy is created and used to create reality.

We told you it was time to stop looking in, or rather, add the outward view to your repertoire. Both are key, but important you understand the power that exists for you to live your energy fully—create it in beautiful, confident ways.

Go full celebration with joy and flecks of light and untethered balloons—all connections to self, others, universe.

Acknowledge it at your fingertips. Use its power of creation for your spirit development.

Look out, look in, look around, look beyond. Look freely with heart wide open. Explore your energy with fanfare.

Describe to those the vision you see. It is a celebration, with loud shouting, streamers, confetti. It that a band I hear?

Boom! It is yours. Can you see that it creates a river that abounds with loving freedom?

Doesn't it feel fabulous to feel the reverberations of the boom, knowing it signals the release of self, enabling the fruitful creation of self?

You are struggling with the explosion metaphor but remember this. Sometimes it takes great power to transform a heart mired in stone. It will survive. Seismic shifts do not come out of polite shakes.

You worry about the destruction imagery, but don't some detrimental structures warrant removal if they block our view.

Contemplate this rather than struggling to change the image.

All those with you are safe. The hatches are battened down. Rather than tiptoe out the door, climb on the rocket and go!

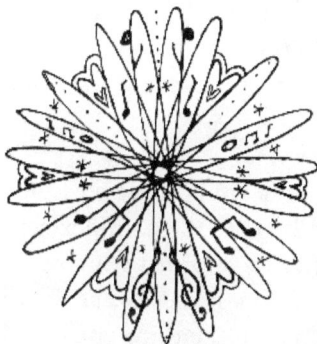

You might be ready to embark on a cosmic journey instead of that little meander you envisioned. Once you lit a fuse of light, you realized a little candle was not enough.

Boom!

Let it happen as a joint venture in divine creation. Power unleashed. Heart exploding in growth and not in destruction, which is a big difference in the use of power.

Transform the energy you used in suppression to energy used in expansion and you will know no bounds in the creation of life that exudes from your heart and through your hands.

Heart alive!

Story in Truth
Reading 3

Insight is useless unless it enters the stream of real time.

Good wonderful day! We welcome you back with arms open to embrace. How open are you? Embrace is two way. You not only receive it but must give it as well.

Which arrives at big questions. How do you open your arms to embrace the world, the people in it, the spirit beyond it? Part of the requirement is that you open to all things—your story, people and their humanness, life as it exists for you in truth.

While you can never fully erase slant, you can strive to eliminate the complex series of curtains, doors, lighting—all the stage props you use to create the story you wish to tell. All our stories are as we wish to tell them, even if we long for them to be different. As the directors of our drama, we have designed everything in the play.

What? But things happened to us! Are we responsible for those damaging events?

Listen to the words. You are wholly responsible for the narrative that springs forth from that. No one is looking to place responsibility on you, the director. We are merely pointing out the telling of the story is in your hands and you do get to tell it as you wish.

Good life/bad life—all those narrators weighing in to tell it your way.

No one is saying bad things did not happen. It is the weaving of the narrative and most importantly, the fullest understanding and acceptance of what was—and is—remains crucial to opening. Do not try to hide it. Condemn it. Praise it. Ignore it. Or revise it. How about you just take a look, nod and accept it?

This leaves you wide open to understanding. It allows you to put it in its rightful place—in your hands without burning them. No guilt required. No revision. No shame. There it is—as it happened—unedited by the voices of protection or condemnation. In your hands does not lend itself to responsibility. No, you are not the cause. Which means you are not the antagonist in the narrative.

Life is a series of events that happen. Humans play out the drama in real time, then spend a significant amount of time and energy editing, judging, revising to fit into other stories that are already recorded. It keeps the narrative going in the direction pre-determined by past decisions—those made behind a curtain, through damaged, tainted eyes.

Pull back the curtain. Try watching the drama with new eyes. What really happened? Is that the story you tell yourself and others or . . . something else?

We maintain a very complex series of shades, curtains and spotlights to tell our stories. Try turning off the lights, pulling back the curtains and lifting the shades. Place yourself in a full spectrum auditorium, just you seated in a surround sound stage with windows all around you and just look, watch as you tell your story now.

Ask yourself—why am I saying that? Who is speaking now? Why have I cut them off or given them center stage? Why is there no joy in this moment? Most importantly, stop looking backward to find the words of the narrative you wish to live now. Try instead to think oh, yes. I see the origins of that, but my perpetually shut arms need to open to embrace a now moment of joy not allowed in this space until I lift the curtain.

Recognize the narrative is all about the past story written, but it doesn't have to be. It never had to be. Hold out your hands and see them as the power directing the story in this moment of breath.

Soon you will see that curtain no longer protects you. It inhibits you from living freely in this moment. Take control of your story. No, rephrase that. Realize you are in control of the telling and always have been—not the events. Yes, you can be the victim of terrible humanity, but you own the hands that create the breathing story that is now!

Close your eyes. Envision the theater in the round with you seated in the middle, spinning in your chair surrounded by windows. Do not live your life here, orchestrating from the chair. Get out of the round and start living. You are not immobile in the chair surrounded by the past events with no escape.

Swiveling and seeing are just the initial steps. This insight is portable. Bring a window with you to glance at in real time when needed. Take it with you tucked in your back pocket— a mini-window of reality for consultation when you want to understand a voice or event from the past.

There is much power in understanding, but far more power in living. Insight is useless unless it enters the stream of real time, in real life, in real actions, basking in real acceptance and love.

Feel the energy in the hands as they construct life events, harnessing the flow of connection and universal energy. That is so much nicer than watching the narrative play out starring chosen narrators of the past.

It's liberating, really, to exit and leave the cumbersome stage equipment behind. It is so much easier to live with window, narrators, memoir tucked neatly in a pocket; real, but shrunken to a manageable size for a continuing journey.

Be careful not to over pack!

Take only what you need for an open, joyous exploration—and nothing more.

Own This Moment
Reading 4

We all dwell in possibility.

Set aside the darkness. Welcome in the light. Spirit lit by candle of joy in pathways of connection. Get into right mind.

First note the floodgates are open, but no flood waters buffet you. All the years, the fears that loosening your grip would set you adrift and you would drown in helpless currents.

Ah, but you did not.

Instead, you opened the door and peered out, walked out, stepped into life's stream and it did not swallow you. Arms wide open. Hands ready to do life. What does that say about you? Your past?

All it says is that you did it that way. You just DID. Everyone just DOES. They live the way that suits their moment in that moment. The only difference is now you realize the moment. You see the moment you are in. You see the play of the moment, the reach of it, the fact it is your life to live.

There is no bemoaning past moments any more than there should be any bemoaning of present moments. You lived then. You live now.

With the light on, you can make your way around the room with new awareness and confidence. Now that you see the moment, you can use your hands to grasp it shape it—own it—instead of using the darkness as shield and using your hands to protect against the tides.

With new eyes you can take stock of the situation and go forth, riding the surf rather than floundering in the flood. So, there you are; new eyes installed, life illuminated, armed with the energy of connection.

Oh, what is the matter? No boom today? Not enough insight for you? Perhaps that is because we are now part of the fabric and this is a time of integration. It no longer seems 'wow' that the new flashes come.

So much revealed. You are both human and divine. All one. Connected widely to all life. Human struggles facilitate soul growth. Hands and eyes are the power of life that illuminate and create.

You have in yourself all that you need—as perfectly flawed being—to live profoundly in the small way of each moment. Gifts abound. Sight. Life. Love. Health. Possibility.

We all dwell in possibility, but we do not always put our foot over that threshold—and yet, when we do, our eyes link to our hearts to set fire to our lives, burning brightly, unafraid of all that living fully entails.

The small and the big are the same. Love and fear are twins. Good and bad are neither. So much to consider in that new wave of life. The possible and the impossible exist in the same space.

Oh, the paradox is all. The paradox is one. Same. Cannot stress too much that all you believed to be true was, but really isn't. Is/Isn't= same.

What to do with that? Get rid of isn't. All things are—as is. Right now. Past is story. Now is breath. Future? Sorry, the wall stops here.

Life exists merely in this moment. Regret is fruitless worry about past desire to change something you can't. Hope is a futile attempt to connect what you do now to an imaginary path out of a desire to control that which is not yours.

Now is your only moment. It is your only gift. It is all you have been given. Live it fully aware and it will joyfully enrich you. It can be a house of mirror for reflection or projection, or it can be vibrant life with soft breezes wafting connection and energy.

You seem disquieted at these revelations. That is because they have settled into you, become part of you. For so long you looked out and learned more about beyond. Now that the beyond has flowed in and become part of your life, the next series will be less about revealing spirit secrets and more about living spirit truths.

If we are indeed one, then we need to thrive in life's moments as they unfold for you. They are now part of the story of your day, rather than being the topic separate from you that awaits your understanding. So much to understand. Time to live!

Time you learn to understand how to LIVE your spirit moments daily. Ponder this shift in reality. No hurry to know more. You need to revel in the moment. Feel the pulse. Live the paradox in each moment.

We are still with you but shift now from seeking to living. Grapple with the fine lines of that.

Paradox again. So vast in the simplest of breaths. Let that wash over you in waves of soft power. Power/love connection one paradox. Take a break. Let all this sink in. Incorporate it. Pause. Woven into the fabric. Enough for now.

Today is Destination
Reading 5

Live this minute in a way that nourishes your spirit.

There really is no such thing as end, transition or beginning.
It is just life lived—process in different shades of change.

Life is always a churn. All you have is just an awareness of
what you can and cannot influence in the process—holding
yourself at the center.

This is me. The changing life events are swirling around me,
but they always do. It is futile to think that all three are not
going on simultaneously at all times.

What does that do to the way you live your life? If you live in
now, what does it matter if some things are ending? Aren't
others beginning? Why should this provoke angst?

It merely is—flow of life.

Only 'control' you have is to open your eyes and make
choices in the moment to . . . what? Live in acceptance of
your moment whatever that has to offer as ending, transition,
start—if those phases even exist! Stops and starts? No! It is
just life in your orbit today. Who knows about tomorrow?

You are a bit too concerned with renovation idea. That
implies it is all in your control and you are in charge of the
hammer and the whole project and that you will be done at
some point creating a life that is more pleasing than the one
you have today.

Look around you. THIS is your life. You may stop living in that house. You may get a new job. Someone may come into your life—or not. See how that focuses on all that which MAY happen? Which may NOT happen?

If/when all those things happen in some imaginary future, they will happen on a day in which your eyes are open and you are breathing in this human incarnation. Until then, continue breathing and seeing and choosing how to live right this minute in a way that nourishes your spirit.

Your sense of time and your control over it is the only thing you need to renovate. Stop thinking 'what kind of life do I wish to create?' Live what kind of life you wish to lead in this moment of time.

Of course, you can plan out your day, week, vacation, life. Just realize it has no power in reality. It is a figment. Nothing more than a hopeful idea—maybe turned into real action, but certainly not powered by your sheer force of will to go the way you wish. Buy the plane ticket now.

Appreciate that moment of joy in anticipating the possibility you will see a loving person in a few weeks but stop thinking you can be happier when you do.

Buying the ticket is the source of happiness. Do not place your happiness on layaway, scrimping and saving and sacrificing until you finally get the means to access it. It is with you right now. Renovate the time/happiness/future thinking.

Life review gives you choices. Living with that insight can bring joy. Dreaming about a happy future is sending your hopes out on air and hoping they will turn into something that will bring you what you have at your fingertips right now.

Bigger questions.

What are you waiting for? Why are you waiting for it?

What enrichment can come to my life in this moment of
decisions with these hands and heart to live in authentic spirit
now. Dreams are not the train's ultimate destination.

Today is.

Body and Spirit
Reading 6

Use your hands to find your own spirit truth.

Good morrow—good day! Good life.

Your work entails the breaking down of the walls, the barriers that you believe separate earth life and spirit life.

Same life. Twins afire.

It is a matter of living life with concrete barriers, glass walls or no separation. Embrace open life in realm of one. That is both. That is one.

See your hands passing through that which exists only from your own construction. All those choices. Thick. Thin. Transparent. Life examined means choosing how to construct barriers, division, protective walls. All of your choosing.

First you looked here. Then you peeked there and you saw link. Then division became apparent and questions arose.

What is the role of these virtual walls we construct in our lives? They are ideas that protect, separate, limit all that we do not wish to understand or see. They are construction. We all build them.

Look.

You are in a body. You are a spirit. How can that not be one? Who do you think you are in body if not a spirit? If your short-term house expires, do you? The body is the ultimate choice of barrier construction. It blends physical limitations with emotional trials and tribulations. It provides limited clarity and short vision eyes into its divine connection. We come here to struggle to see a range of truth not evident if either side is alone.

If you focus only on worldly, you miss the importance of spirit. If you reside mainly in spirit, you miss the truth and boundless nature of human experience; the beauty of fresh air, the buzz of the bee, a soft kiss.

Your challenge—can you widen your sight to embrace both in total glory?

Appreciation of one should only enhance the depth of value you can see in the other.

Pure spirit truth embraces life here in all its incarnations and flourishes there in growth of divine nature.

And yet the walls . . . oh, the construction.

Their dissolution, their deconstruction generates the energy that fuels our journey towards our own divine nature and its place in the grander divine.

You are here to breathe deeply, to learn much about self and spirit. Fuse that vision into a unified belief that dissolving walls enhances vision and fosters connection in our slow dance toward divine light. It cannot happen in darkness.

There is a question to ask self at all times. How does this help me grow in spirit, because if you do that while in body you will expand your understanding of grander truth.

Do your choices build or remove walls? Building walls never enhances your insight. They may protect, but they will never produce light, only darkness.

Soul challenge is to create light. Seek light. Gravitate toward guiding light in true loving action. That is not a journey easy in darkness. Your journey here is really a soul journey, so use your body in the moment of now to flood your experiences with light and your travels will take you places of greatness unfettered and unshielded by walls, dark shadows and fears.

Godspeed in your journey forth. You have been given hands, the tools of construction and deconstruction and they are yours to use this time around in ways ultimately of your choosing.

Tools of truth in light, or tools of constructing darkness? Your choice as you breathe in this divine moment.

Is it an accident you have two of them? Ponder that. They work in tandem to create human and spirit light. Yin/yang.

Paradox in their power to create light and dark in two realms—power untapped in simplistic, paired beauty. Not accidentally two as one.

Nothing is accidental.

There exists a vast range seen in either/or paradox. Embrace life pulsing in cells and in God. Reconcile that and human/spirit one is easier to see. If those can come from same life force, so can you!

Use your hands to find your own spirit truth. No one can give that truth to you.

Align Micro/Macro
Reading 7

The soul place and the human place are the same place.

People do not renovate to create a better future.

They renovate to make the now they have more suitable to their true nature. Renovation is the act of creating now in alignment with your authentic soul self in an attempt to align human with authentic self.

Deconstructing walls both dividing and linking human and authentic self will allow you to unite as one.

You need to live with self in totality, which requires the alignment of the micro and the macro—that which is between earth and body and between earth and spirit.

The soul place and the human place are the same place.

The theme is alignment. It is impossible to perceive ONE without it.

Cleave One Breath

Can soul and human be cleaved in this one breath?

Good morrow. Breathe deeply and let the cool breeze wash over you. Hear the birds chirping their song to the universe. It is a beautiful statement of fact. I am here. I am living.

Time is our topic. Examine all the terms you use to describe it.

To truly see its value, you must dig into how you view it, which reveals so many ways to shape our perceptions of it: past, present, future, plan, reflect, breathe, progress, regress.

We could brainstorm hundreds of those words to show our thinking. Our past happened as a result of factors in and out of our control and our challenge at this moment is to use that information to create a better future.

This places our hopes and dreams at a point out of our grasp. It is a point we live for, plan for, control for. Interesting how much of that scenario gives power to the irrelevant and devotes almost no time to the only thing relevant to the life you have, which at this moment is the breeze and the birds.

If only . . . because . . . are two detrimental terms the thwart our efforts at living fruitfully.

I can't _____ because_____. Fill in the blank: my abusive childhood, the weather. There are infinite cannots in the world.

There are elements of truth in them, of course. You can't buy the jet. Perhaps you do carry a lot of emotional baggage on your journey. All true.

But does skipping over now by working on plans to get 'there' make any of it closer to authentic soul happiness?

Examine words 'working on' and 'progress'. What do these do for your soul fulfillment if all activity goes in the 'development' bin?

There is only one bin. It is labeled NOW.

Your baggage resides with you now. Your flawed spouse, children, circumstances, life, all reside with you now. Does that preclude you from feeling the breeze of life wafting on your neck or tousling your hair?

Examine all your time thoughts for degrees of past or future displacement. Those all reside in the now bin, so don't think sorting them and putting them into their rightful place matters.

How you live is a compilation of soul self and life experiences, all of which mesh into the face you see in the mirror every morning, every minute you have. Yes, you can renovate your life to live fulfilled in soul awareness, but you cannot live your life to be more soulfully authentic in some ill-defined future.

This is it. Your view of yourself and your perception of your gifted time are all that matters. Right now, your only question in the air is how to live soulfully, today—in alignment of soul and human. That is NOT a goal. That is your reality.

Any unhappiness you feel is disparity when your human incarnation and your authentic soul are cleaved (divided) instead of cleaved (bonded).

To what degree can this one word with opposite meanings describe the soul/human paradox? It perfectly describes the paradox that faces us as we live here now.

Can soul and human be cleaved/united in this one breath?

One. One you. One moment. One soul living this time as is. One breath. One breeze. One hope you will unite with the divine through embracement of all that pulses in life— and really the only thing that pulses with life.

Your heart center is key to that. It keeps you alive. It connects you to all. It streams energy to the divine.

Feel that breeze? Let it stream through your heart and into your spirit and into your life and into the universe that links to divine truth.

The smallest and the largest, all perched in this moment of truth—life possibility is progress while not moving, just heart pulsing now. That is the grandest paradox of all—not just for you and spirit one. All life divine one.

One.

How wide can your arms spread to embrace that idea? Pry your mind open first and your heart will be free to follow. Do not let ego have too much say here. It is loudly human and likes to dominate the conversation, but it is only half the story. Yes, I hear you, BUT there is a whisper I need to attend to, a message I need to hear.

One. Allow the human in you to hear spirit as it calls out to you. Chirping away.

I am here. I live too.

Perfect in Place
Reading 9

Relish the audacity of living fully.

Ah, hello busy one.

All the dominoes in a row, moving down the line; notice the motion in your life—and yet, no seeming movement. Growth in place, opening standing still.

You are still standing in place and yet—can you see the arms unwrap their protective crouch and open wide to the world— a bigger embrace—a removal of walls to protect you?

Walls to protect also isolate and restrict. It is impossible to embrace through a wall.

So, embracement. I know. Not a common word, but it can be if you want it to describe how it feels to reach out and breathe life in—wrap your arms around it in joy—open. I can live this life!

Stop thinking about how much you have to learn. Let's focus on how much you have to <u>feel</u>—feel life! Feel energy! Feel human connection and emotion.

You keep looking through the crack in the door and seeing the beauty for a moment. Then it slams shut. It is so big! You are not ready.

Once you fling the door open be prepared for floodgates. That is what you are preparing for. That glimpse of the universe you saw through the records can be here, too, and embraced in earthly beauty.

Because as you know through your study, there are many sides to everything that unites in one. Full circular view requires you to see both the universe beyond here and the universe here as lived in a truly open dimension beyond the view of every day.

You will be astonished. Not too much study is required—just you living bigger spirit life as human.

There is nothing to fear. Make room in your heart to love in constant expansion while perfect in place as is.

Be it. Accept it. It is knowable. Feel-able. Livable in spirit whether there is a body to deal with or not.

Do you have the capacity to see it all? What do you believe this is all for? We are inviting you in our gentle embrace, preparing you to see the astonishing and relish the audacity of living fully—no, not to 'accomplish' much and to scale adventurous mountains, but to swoop through life on the winds of a spirit. Feel the energy seep in through every pore. You can feel it just sitting here. This is your divine life seen through human eyes and felt through a divinely human heart.

Simply put, complexity and simplicity exist in all.
    Love—simple/complex
    People—simple/complex
    Life—simple/complex
    Lessons—simple/complex

Strive to accept the complex and the simple in one embrace. As you gaze around and feel the teeming life in this simple of places, the enormity should impress you. The simplicity should inspire you. The flow should energize you as it carries you along the path to your enlightenment.

Vacillate between "Oh my God!" and "I'm okay with that." Side by side they make truth—awesome truth.

Yours to feel with arms wide open.

See the Wonder
Reading 10

We stop running after the wonder.

A child runs unfettered, unconcerned with doing it right. He just runs joyously toward the duck he will never catch.

You can, too.

Is it the duck, or the joy of running that matters? The child never once ponders the possibility of 'failure' to catch the duck. He just breaks free of Dad's hand, then takes off! The stick along the way distracts too, but how interesting to bang that on something then on to the next adventure.

When do we lose that? We stop running after the wonder—toward the wonder—stepping on the stick and moaning at its hurt. Ouch! Perhaps we lose it when Dad stops following behind and the hurt becomes ours and not his.

Running the gauntlet alone is not so fine. Maybe we give up too soon and forget to trust the world and the see the wonder in it all.

Creation of Purpose
Reading 11

Reside in the blank space of possibility.

Greetings again.

Long, but oh so interesting pause. Would you agree?

Thank you for your attention to ritual—like you are focusing in important ways on this connection. But you do realize that is for you—and not us?

Whatever gets you here. Good!

So, today we wish to talk about explorations of the heart, by the heart, for the heart—using your heart as guide to developing the heart at the center of all life.

That uplifting draft you are feeling is the winds of change sweeping through your heart—healing it, enriching it, nourishing it.

You, of course, picture the heart chamber as an open-air porch. The locked sides are finally lifted. It is currently empty of all but that life-renewing breeze that is whooshing over you. This is the medicine of an open heart.

The ritual, the human emotion. All are superseded by this. You have dared to find this place and here is the connection you craved. Answers? This is the answer to question of purpose. You can safely reside here and the winds of the moment will caress you. Value this above all else. In this empty space you are seeing it all—and feeling the gentle breeze of spirit.

It looks empty because it is the moment. It waits for divine creation of action in your hands. This is moment envisioned in life. Reside in the blank space of possibility in each moment.

It is untainted, wide-open opportunity that is not concerned with past or future. The breeze washes over you in now and you are free to make it what you wish to experience—from grand gestures to letting the bird chirps nourish you. You saw the grand in the universe. Remember the library, the open walls, the vast connections, the spiritual?

This is its mirror, no?

This is the human moment, the earth side of that vision. Merge them into one vision if you can. Right now. You are just discovering spirit heart is one with human heart. Soon, those two can become one.

That vast landscape can and will become that one moment. They are same, just decorated differently with your heart laid bare to live in both. The more you explore both realms, the more they will seem less 'connected' and more just the same realm.

Know this:
Your life is eternal, and you have been granted vision to see oneness. This is bestowed on you by the winds of the moment but use it to live richly in that moment and not for some future sharing. Like ritual, sharing feeds the human side of you, but is not at all relevant to our conversation.

One.
Heart.
Links all.

There is no true barrier to the channel that flows through body/spirit life other than the limits our circumstances (body, brain, life) present.

Deconstruct those and you will participate in that open energy carried in currents that flow freely and reside in that open space free of incarnation and steeped in spirit.

There it is.

Here it is.

Divine heart.

Pulsing at this moment—in you.

Opening Patient Eyes
Reading 12

Stop looking to others to tell you how to be in spirit realm.

Greetings!

Well, shall we talk about patience? We patiently wait while you go through your rituals—as unnecessary as they are for us—very much for you.

Humans trying to make sense of that beyond their comprehension, but so integral a part of them it cannot be denied.

We are patient with you. You must be patient with yourself and with all others in your scope.

What does that mean? Triangulate your position. Most people have been given one set of eyes. They look outward, mostly, trying to make sense of what they see around them. Although they sense something (a longing) in them, they keep looking outside themselves for the sense—a ray of light—a knowing.

But their eyes look more out than in. This is a draw to common thinking of the group—answers that others around them can affirm—a balm, mayhap. It works for them in constructing narrative, making sense of painful, confusing world.

Some eyes are different. At first you tried to control this narrative by saying two sets, but really it is just one that works differently. They see both ways, giving multiple views of every situation.

They are not perfect eyes. They may see things, but maybe not as clearly as they think they do. You are a storyteller, too, but your stories tell a different tale. Your eyes see your stories and the layers of stories around you, including beyond the external. The internal, too.

Struggling for the metaphor because not much on earth has this double vision—telescopes see the wide, external view and microscopes see the minute, internal workings.

Few humans see as such and they reside in small space. The vast majority don't want to peer in, or should we say they are seeking to gain insight through their telescopes, thus the cosmic view of religion and ritual and groups of like-minded thinkers.

But enough about them. What about you?

Can you accept this about yourself and stop worrying about being arrogant or judgmental? Better yet, stop being arrogant and judgmental.

Verify and accept your place as observer with different vision. Stop trying to hear spirits of people past. Stop trying to find a tribe with the same vision. Your whole life you have looked to others to guide who you should be. How to be a better teacher, parent, spouse, person. That was to help you cope better as human.

But as you become more of yourself as unique spirit in human incarnation, stop looking to others to tell you how to be in spirit realm. Your attempts are making you doubt who you are, implying if you only knew more you would be a 'better' spirit.

How about you just be who you are?

Not saying you can't be open to learning how others do it. Of course, you may remain open to learning more to enrich your own development but stop thinking you need to do what others do.

Appreciate the sight you have been given. Use it to remain open to our guidance and intervention. Yes, you can enrich your spiritual practice if/when it speaks to you but if ritual does not do it for you, use your sight to wish others well in their pursuit.

Have the patience to allow others to proceed on their paths but open your heart to allow that patience for yourself. You will unfold in your own time, in your own way with an open heart and powerful, insightful eyes.

Do not use the vision observations you see of others taint your vision of yourself. Patiently watch, observe, listen and you will blossom in your own way in your own time.

The theme of your narrative is openly patient. We are that with you and all others, waiting patiently in the blank space to welcome authentic you into....

What? Into what?

Patience, my dear. That is for another day! Ha!

Holes and Vistas
Reading 13

This is a solo performance of soul.

Grand morning—grand hello.

We welcome you back. The entrance is yours when you want it—gate sits quietly here, waiting for you to enter at your will.

And please know it is you who enters each time. You are struggling with thoughts of constructed self, authentic self. All along we have urged you to broaden your vision to embrace all possibilities.

You keep saying you do not know authentic self. Yet, there she is, part you as spirit, part you human wounded—part you constructed safe guardian—all you—blind eye turned to obvious. This is all you. Stop looking for a bifurcation. Where does constructed you begin, dominate and where does soul-self reside. Who is she, really?

Yes, we say. She is all that—and more.

Quit chopping up, dissecting the pieces. This does you no good. Your goal/job is to knit those self-imposed pieces together into lovely quilt of reality. You are you in all these glorious pieces. The soul helps with human construction; therefore, it reveals much about the soul. So instead of pondering this and wringing your hands, use the hands to bind the pieces together. Live more as human to find soul parameters of that line; more as soul to see how human shaped by spirit.

Expand view of whole. You have been told this before. We repeat. Expansion requires inclusion of human and soul in unison as one. Those protective guardian voices have much to offer you in strength. You have much to offer them in humanity. You have the hands right now to sew the quilt and design it and admire it and appreciate it for its beauty and comfort.

And please, do not shut out these voices reaching out to you. They offer much and should not be measured in comparison to anyone else's experience but your own. Let them sprinkle salt if that brings them to a place of openness—or, brings them to a place of delusion. No one else's experience matters here. We talk to you. Stop judging others—and yourself—by the other voices in the choir.

This is a solo performance of soul. You are charged with your own development for now. Trust you have it in you to find the peace of truth and stop creating the churn and doubt that erodes the soul.

It was time to move on. What a wonderful examination of human life you did. The knowledge revealed should be used in honor of soul expansion.

Digging deeper into the well of human pain not needed at this time, but do not discount the possibility in the future. You know it is there. You understand many of its parameters. It is the other squares on the quilt that now require your embellishment. Use your understanding of past to enlighten your choices in real time, but do not dwell forever in dark places as there is limited light to be shed by peering there. The true sharp, beautiful light exists outside of that human misery and in corners/activities spiritual. Time to turn the spotlight there.

You excavated caves. Now explore the mountains and the vista they provide—realizing they both are integral to the other—and both occupy the same space.

The walls/rocks/obstacles that divide them are hardened by despair, so do not allow that to rule the day of exploration—all reside in same space. Your choice is not to retell a palatable narrative but to see a wider view of life that enables you to flourish with a wider vision.

Rise up and out. Acceptance is when you can strive to see it all. It isn't when you give up looking—a very important distinction to consider.

So yes, it is up to you. No one else can do this for you. The call of the cardinal in its real glory is for you—not disconnected and not alone—but you, who requires a wider vision to see the awe at hand.

You have work as human to do, yes, but look at it in its entirety as soul work, too. Actually, it is all soul work as living as human gives the opportunity to challenge and grow or bury and deny.

But it matters naught for others in your lens. It is your lens. Your life. Your soul opportunity. Your vision, colored by despair or encompassing unending potential—life, beauty at the birdfeeder in smallest beating heart—and in you. Beating in you.

Eyes ablaze or eyes closed.

Your eyes. Only your eyes.

See what you will.

Good luck!

Eternal Light Force
Reading 14

Light reveals what secrets exist in full view.

What a jumble as we tumble around in greeting. So happy to be with you again. Revived light force/heart-human.

Greetings!

We did not lose heart even when you seemed to—but your heart rested there in waiting, cloaked in uncertainty. Wondering when again the song would call for it.

Well, it is now.

Fling off the dark cover of protection you used to shield you from doubts and questions. Where does this reside? What is the source of the spring? It is as you know it. It is eternal life force, power through eternity that flows from one to the other through time, places, people, bodies, lives, dreams of humanity. All those separations do not exist in reality. At least not in permanent, divine way. You sought to pretend you do not know what you know. Threw a shroud around the light because your questions drown out your truth in a short cacophony of ego snapping at your heels, eating your heart, shadowing your reality.

Enough of dwelling there. What is new to know, understand, grasp, grapple open?

Let the light in. Yes, light.

The flame of you uniquely sits patiently in your center, waiting to be what it is meant to be, which is truly you, connected to all—illuminated inside and out—a beacon, really, of how to follow the steps into fruition and fulfillment of soul self.

You can see it there. Little flicker. That is you as you exist in time. You keep bombarding us with questions. What do I do with it? Grow it? Hold it? Your task is to see it. Know it. Discover its value in perfect splendor. Cradle it. Caress it. Live it. Just live it. Put it front and center. Hold it in your hands. Your heart. Your soul. Enjoy the central nature of something so simple being there.

It is you. Beautiful. Strong. Unique. Perfect in its entirety. But it is a shared flame so we go back to the ideas of one and connection and paradox with you.

It is one. It is you. It is all life force glowing with eternal divinity. Connects all. Entirely, uniquely you. How can all this be? If you can accept this vision of simple light within you as most powerful force in the world.

Can you not accept that all life's contradictions are not opposites? They do not negate one another. In fact, they flesh out the true complexity, intricacy with which we live.

Many truths—one.

Many souls—one.

Many lights—one.

Your soul as you—your soul deeply meshed with others.

So, what to do with vision of small flame, insignificant grandeur beyond comprehension. All you can do is marvel at how light must be taken as is to embrace vastness. Simplicity. Simply let the pilot light burn simple in all things in many ways.

Ember, flame, illumination, strength, hope, acceptance. It is all of these in and beyond you.

You determine its place, sphere. It burns no matter what. So, when it goes dark, look to what you have tossed over it as shroud and why. When it glows alone, appreciate its steadfastness while moving around to see another side of the prism.

It is. What you do with it is you.

Light reveals what secrets exist in full view.

Oh, life's true call in human incarnation is how to create metaphor to grasp soul that is vast beyond full comprehension.

Listening with Spirit
Reading 15

Listen with spirit ears.

Salutations.

Envision us gathered around you ready to share a message for you, yet just through you. Notice how many times you are in a situation to share.

Feel your way around that. Open. What to do with it?

Great topic of examination to continue. We have given you today's topic, so listen rather than pondering, searching that brain of yours. Sharing.

What does it mean to share?

We are sharing with you. The most simplistic thought is it means to give something, but you know, of course, nothing is that simple. In joining the continuity of spirit, remember sharing is not just one way when you are giving something. So, as you sit in presence, do not always focus on what wisdom or insight comes clearly to you. Yes, you are receiving insight, but what you have failed to grasp is that receiving and sharing flow in both directions.

Since we often close off for protection, we shut that door and open the giving door which really shuts off half of the power.

As always, we remind you to listen, but remember ears are just physical body parts that detect sound. You need to let that sound enter your ears, mind, then heart. You are not being sent into these situations to talk or to even gather information. Yes, that is part of it. But open-hearted listening requires you to take in the flow in an entirely beyond physical, intellectual level.

Instead, what soul messages are being shared with you that you are hearing through sound, detaching and processing through intellect and storing in the archives of your mind to be applied to practice? Again, how does this pertain to you that you can share with others?

NO! Stop that! You are missing huge opportunity at own soul growth by listening to spirit exchanges through filtered, human ears and responding with ego driven answers. When people are talking spirit to spirit, listen with spirit ears and spirit heart. Open doors of floodgates to two-way sharing accepted in heart for mutual enlargement. That is the point you have been missing.

Your worry of oversharing stems from this. In practice you guard self, listen, record, then provide feedback in very limited closed loop.

Acknowledge the spirit wisdom of those speaking, rather than the ideas that connect solidly to your already ideas. Sit in spirit when the ego is in charge of the ears and the doors and the protections.

Have a little chat before opportunity arises and confirm the fears, assure human side of self that such enlargement will benefit all. No need to worry about judgment or attack, so open to spirit flow entering your spirit heart connection. Welcome ego observer but relieve it of its protective duty and enlarge it to watch and perhaps heal and grow in the warmth of spirit light development.

Perhaps that is the ultimate sharing and peace that must go on. Put to rest your ego's push to have its say, to protect you, to guide your vision. Sharing a goal of enlargement unites your soul and your humanity in common quest of a better incarnation and ultimately wider expanse of soul development while here.

So, sharing key to expansion. Listen to the wisdom of those around you and share experiences in soul expansion.

Unite the divided factions of your own incarnation and share space—ego and spirit—which can both reside in and benefit from joint agreement to grow.

Sharing requires the transformation of walls into energy connections that feed the flowing expansion of spiritual self.

Listening is one way. Sharing is two way. Connections require a holistic view of peace with self and others that nurtures and develops your place in the universal as the divine intends for all souls. You are seeing connection as we speak.

Take a snapshot of this image of you sharing spirit in the universe—true connection with divine alive in you!

Let your eyes and ears remain open to what you have just seen and heard. Try to replicate that open connection as you move through your journey. It is only selfish if you seek to dispense rather than absorb and expand.

Such a revolution of spirit!

The Alchemist's Eyes
Reading 16

The purpose of every quest is new sight.

Do not worry overmuch about creating the conditions for conversation. We are here always. Waiting patiently—always—for you to join us in an exchange of ideas about....

Ah, there you have it. About what?

In your mind, the racing is for the right topic to consider.

There it is again. Well, shall we say instead that every one of our encounters is about seeing? Living is about seeing. All of life is about taking in the energy life force that flows in all forms. Here you see it with your eyes, but we ask that you do two things.

"See" it with other paths as well. See with your heart. See with your fingers, mind, spirit—and please put the word new with that. New Sight.

The purpose of every quest is new sight. Each day presents you with a fresh set of eyes to see new in front of you, around you, beyond you. To continuously enlarge spirit, you must always look at the world in new ways, even if nothing new presents itself within your line of sight.

This does not mean you must venture forth to see all the different earth has to offer. This is not a journey of the restless. It is a voyage of the patient.

New can be in your surroundings or your mind or your heart—your insight, your understanding of all the richness that envelopes you here and there. You can be trapped in the well and keep looking at the darkness no matter where you are—or you can live and breathe with a sense of wonder for the complexity and simplicity that create this being and the journey of all beings.

New sight is joyous sight because tucked behind each corner is the path of expansion and your soul can grow to fit the boundaries of whatever sight lines you choose to construct. It is all in you and beyond you and somehow those two ideas should become one as everyday becomes a new day—every day.

Although please do not fret that one must live in a constant state of epiphany. How exhausting that would be! While those sparks are lovely, do not feel like the rest of life falls short in its ordinary. As you embrace new sight, paradox resides in all other life. You have been given that time and again and again and again. There is new spark in epiphany. There is great expansion in living with new sight of the ordinary.

Nothing is all this or that which should be your newest sight of all. How rich is simply breathing in the day, taking in all the sides and watching your soul expand and create life force from nothing.

Alchemy, really.

No brass bands. No fanfare necessary. In each day lies the magic opportunity of new sight and spirit development. Do not squander it if you can help it, but no pressure to go at any pace.

This is just a gift we hold out to you from our hearts. Take it into your hands and place it in your own heart and see how the light of new vision flows from you in rivers of growth.

The words are failing you now because you are feeling instead, so remember to expand your grasp of sight beyond your eyes and appreciate all the paths that flow through you towards enlightenment. Keep pushing your constructed boundaries, knowing it is beyond anything you can fathom.

So much to see. So much to expand. Boundless spirit comes alive when you open your being in new ways to see and embrace all that is around you.

Cosmic embrace. Infinite expansion.

Wow!

PS- Psychology is spirit development described in human terms. It defines your story so you can grasp how it was written and take control of the narrative to guide the expansion of your spirit. It makes you cognizant of the circumstances behind your story and how it was being written either for you or by you. Psychology allows you to take ownership of the pen that records your story and you can tell the tale as constricted or expansive as you desire, but it without a doubt, your soul's journey to tell.

The winds don't stop blowing, but at the helm you own the adventure rather than just getting buffeted by the gale.

Embrace 360° Theater

Reading 17

Open the door to accepting the incredible.

Tap. Tap. Tapping on your shoulder.

We are here. You are opening. Do not miss this opportunity to expand.

Looking 360° now. As you balance and teeter and spin on the life wheel, do not despair of looking back, making future better. Change, swirl.

You lie at the center of all. It swirls around you. You are not really part of the current that moves the pieces around you and through you. You are at the center.

Envision a beating heart/soul lying still in the center of a pulsing universe—objects, ideas, people, life surging all around you.

Take it all in. You are not spinning. All the other things are and you can watch, look and listen.

The past is in full view. The present incarnation as human. The energy flow that carries you into expansion. They are not different times. They are now, part of your story of the records as you stand still and gently turn around you can accept the notion that all life is reduced to this—your soul/body's moment in now.

The essence you carry with you and have placed temporarily in this body is unwavering and true. Central question—why? Pain. Emotion. Physical challenges. Spirit. Intuition.

Connection. All are expansion of soul self toward the divine light that illuminates all energy with truth.

It is vast. Your whole experience of soul development is so vast it is beyond the comprehension of that which you are right now. So, why unite soul with body? Why narrow the lens to see only through the tiny dot of a microscope?

Well, it makes the vast manageable, within reach. You can focus in on the pieces of healing expansion and making them real through action—completely—in the smallest of cells to get a taste of the vast universe it reflects. Science/spirit/human/explorations all a piece of the quest, a desire to understand that which is bigger than the eye.

Would you believe you are bigger than what your senses tell you if you did not have these QUESTIONS? All these questions to ask in real time, to hold in your hands, smell and taste; corporeal experiences to process as answer.

So, as you sit in central viewing area of 360° theater unfolding around you in multiple layers of time, recognize the beauty of the quest and the essential nature of the questions that pass by in the flurry of activity. They open us to expansion of divine opportunities presented at same time vast and small, divine and human, past and present, you and all those not you but connected.

Embrace it all as best you can through the small eyes gazing through a small microscope of a vast tableau that embraces and explains all. That glimpse is your invitation to a grand spectacle of life, including and beyond that which you know to be true.

Sit for a moment and envision it.

Place you at the center, then look all around. Here you are right now—surrounded by pulses of light and energy—events in the past, earthly life circumstances and light flashes you have yet to experience. All in motion. Layered. Vibrant. You are able to see in front, behind, beyond, connected by life force.

The purpose of this vision? It should allow you the opportunity to open the door to accepting the incredible and incomprehensible, to see the beauty and truth in all of it; especially in all that is you. You are not a flawed, struggling human in this scenario.

You are existing in a moment of spiritual beauty and expansion in constant movement toward divine knowledge that is yours, too.

Envision your place in all of it and you will be filled with the power of acceptance—and joy.

The pulse of this moment is yours to embrace.

Divine connection.
Divine acceptance.
Yours.

Too vast for more words, really.

This is a feeling, not an explanation.

Co-Create Destiny
Reading 18

It is you who creates the energy path.

Return to the library of all time and gaze around you as you did that first time. It is still as spectacular as ever. Remember the awe?

Now it is time to share and help others remember it too. We have given these to you as gifts to you. Your now-eyes are different from your then-eyes and your soul/earthly understanding has expanded.

What does it mean to be a soul longing to know and love divine and self as one? What is it to be human and experience both the beauty and the pain in body? But most importantly, embrace all facets, how it all beats with the same divine heart. You and your body with the divine and all others, pulsing with spiritual truth no matter where and what.

To state—those ideas to grasp—

Expansion is the ultimate goal of spiritual development. Expand in love to mesh into one with the divine. Humanity is one vehicle. It exposes you to others and through them you can begin to know soulful you, connected to self, one, all, divine in love. And how does pain lead us there?

It is through pain that we see not pain and when we can embrace that pain is inherent in life, we remove its power to restrict and to hurt. When we accept it as such, as is, we can see how it pales beyond other powerful forces that reside in same space and then you can see love, hope and expansion as connecting us to divine. It all connects us to divine.

Though we have been given power as cocreators, we fail to use this power if we allow ourselves to succumb to pain, to be ruled by darkness, to only see that which hurts or restricts. We must also be wary of flimsy paint that covers pain but does not heal. The failure to peer behind the sunny curtain also robs us of full-view living required in expansion.

Look beyond the pain, look beyond the false optimism. Look instead at the coexistence of the vast. It is where you truly reside as spirit in human/human with soul—painful and joyous—both struggling and powerful enough to expand beyond the boundaries you have been given.

Or have you constructed them? Do they build around you or within you? Only you have the power to co-construct the answer to that one.

Underneath it all, at the heart of what you must all do; find you and agree to take on the role of co-creator in your destiny beyond this breath. It is a much more infinite creating than our human minds can grasp, which is why you need to bond the human and the spirit as one together in the quest of creation—unity with divinity.

Find your heart beating in body and in spirit and see it as the power link to expansion within your reach as life pumps through you it is both body and spirit. As your breath flows in and out it is also spirit in body.

So, in answer to your question, what should you do next, the answer remains the same.

Expand your vision, your activities in divine pursuits of body and spirit. How you do that with your body and spirit is your portion of the co-creation.

We sit here in truth, unwavering and unchanging. It is you who creates the energy path, so the answer is really yours.

What should you do with this discovery of divine spiritual co-creator in search of divine expansion?

Why are you asking us? We cannot give you that answer. It is up to you to create it.

Power of Yet
Reading 19

To what end?

Knock. Knock. Knock. Knock. Hello. Hello.

You are feeling the infusion of our light—so many topics to address—but let us slow down this moment a bit and breathe. No one says today is the day to address all. Today is the day of beginning to look while open, finally open a bit, to the world, to the universe, to the energy, to yourself.

We have confined your vision to a pinprick at this point and now you think you see a window instead. But what if there was NOTHING to restrict you—not walls, not glass, not earthly relationships? What if there was just you, spirit in body in charge of deciding parameters?

You are indeed the definer of all limits, both earthly and spiritual. Deliberately choose them, but always acknowledge a choice is at hand—your hand, your heart, your spirit wrought everything you create and thereby encounter for yourself. Of course, not for others, but for yourself only. As you swim in the ocean the life teams around you, but you have agency of place in time and space, so courageously and confidently take life into your hands. Reconcile past with current, then take the wheel and guide yourself into your path of currents—future resolution. Pivot point. So full of the moment of possibility.

Take stock. What have you learned about yourself? How much is authentic self? Earthly constructed self? But here is that. That construction is entirely yours. Yes, what happened did happen, but you constructed the memories, the response, the impact. You assigned the influence it has over your present breath. Regrets? Entirely yours. Memories? Constructed using bonsai clippers. Impact? That is well as within your power to do so.

Question. How much does it matter now? How it mattered in the past matters naught. How the past matters is totally yours to bear, so bear it courageously and confidently. Do not draw the curtains to shy away.

The vision you have is the past, now and beyond the moment of now on earth. Send the tentacles of power out and take control of where they were, what and where they are and where they will grow. Take stock now.

It is time to do so before fully taking the reins. No. That taking stock IS fully taking the reins. Own your life. Own the past of it. Breathe the present of it. Guide the future of it in tandem with the power of connection now gifted to you by spirit, empowered by infused light and love.

Capture what you know in all its reality. Use your hands—connected to your heart, flowing into your spirit that flings out into the universe with wild abandon—funneled inward and outward through your hands. Remember that.

Take stock of the construction of past and present.

You keep trying to steer this conversation in the direction you would like it to go, so let us pause. Interesting co-creation. Can we work together to proceed as co-creators, not just us flowing message through you.

Why yes, of course. What about yet?

Remember. Restrictions are of your determination, so up to you how to deconstruct and construct any of this restriction of past and present thinking. We have told you, it is up to you. The power of yet lies entirely in your hands. It is up to you to determine when you are ready. How you are ready. Best use of life breath, best use of connection to spirit.

Key question of yet—to what end? To enrich your soul? To connect to divine light? To help others do so?

You are called by your soul to do your soul's work. You have yet to find key, so work on that first. Teacher. Writer. Nurturer. Wounded child. Faulty human. Beautiful spirit. Come to terms with it, then return to that question. To what end?

Comfort people? Gently help them along their own spiritual path? Provide insight into what they hunger for, but cannot see? Who should help you in this endeavor? Is there a connection to spirit waiting patiently for you to ask? Have you fully nurtured your access to those able to help and guide you? No, you have not.

In your expanding sense of power, refrain from over-seeing it. You are an infant in this, with much to do, so much YET to develop:
1) Examine and define your soul self.
2) Look at spirit—past as human.
3) Look at spirit—past as spirit.
4) Look outward at expanding, strengthening your connection to spirit with more deliberate engagement.
5) Then look at what yet awaits in answer to question, to what end?

Swirling around you in this whirlwind of muddled excitement there is clarity and soul fulfillment. You must do the work to identify, understand, develop, harness and expand to help soul flourish in light—co-created by human hand and spirit power divine.

Dissolve the divide that hinders sight—blinding or enlightening—your choice.

Seeing is not a thing you just do. It, as in all verbs in life experiences, requires choices. Its power lies in creation. We see the wheels of human brain tumbling about as you seek understanding of this.

We are just smiling. There is enormous responsibility in human hands.

Good luck!

1,001 Layered Stories

Reading 20

The human is such a fantastic alchemy of contradiction.

Scheherazade,

Yes, that is what we meant. A name—a magical utterance, a mysterious energy here to guide you today. Comment on all your work. Look at the pathways before you—oracles, tarot, candles, books, advice . . . a hundred and one tales to tell in stories that unfold in revealing ways.

All trappings you do not need but can be used to serve as tangible earthly to universal spiritual—a conduit of focus if you will, so use them if you like. They can take what you have and put it in your hands—focus—to make the energy real to you. It is anyway but do whatever it takes to continue your expansion into the light.

So much bombardment now. Channels coming at you at all times. Don't forget you are in body, too. There is a richness to experience that spirit needs to expand. It is not an either/or choice. There you go for today.

We go back to paradox. This time expand that idea beyond it can be this or that. There is no this or that. It is all in a unit, multifaceted and all true. One. A concept we have mentioned before and now offer up for re-examination with a bigger heart and improved understanding of story possibilities.

Before you are examples all around. The spirit of the light and the dark, the heart of good and evil. The human is such a fantastic alchemy of contradiction.

The spirit is as mysterious and veiled as it is obvious. Mysteries of opposites abound but try to see beyond the bifurcation of what appears to be contradictions. Nothing is really contradictory at all. At any time in any place it can be all at once and many things at the same time. One can be many. All can be singular. Human and spirit can be diverse, separate, united and same.

All at once.

That is the nature of the quest you seek. Seeing all that is in all-spectrum ugliness and beauty, on one plane and on many.

When you live life this way, your interactions with the world and all in it expands beyond the moment into the infinite and you can be human and spirit existing in same breath, occupying same space.

This can temper the minute and put the infinite within your grasp, merged into a single view that accepts all while working toward betterment through expansion. You can see it but see beyond it. You can accept it but move to improve it.

What you should not do is dissect it to pass judgment about the value, goodness, efficacy, reality of any other being or any situation.

Your earthly provides a view of the universe. Your spirit provides you a glorious tableau of the earthly. Live it all— within and beyond the moment, with the flaws and the flawless. You can be both at the same time. Perfectly imperfect.

Sit with that view while you make sense of it. The protons and the neutrons are integral to eternity. So mind boggling to envision the vastness of this truth—all the layers—the size of the one and there you are somewhere thriving in the layers with you a microcosm of that—both minute and vast at the same time. A thousand and one layers of stories in which you exist.

This message is for you—to share will just be to launch it into what you are already part of—into the waiting hands of those who have wondered—get another human (like the cards and the readings) to provide a tether from the earth to the infinite—and hope to use it as a conduit for their own exploration abroad.

Gather close, clarify, expand. Gifts have been given and you have developed them over eons. We lifted the veil so you could peek—look deep into your soul and into the vast beyond and use this vision to enlarge yourself—microscope/telescope. One tool. Same goal. Yes.

There you have it for now.

Isn't that enough?

More. More. More implies this isn't enough.

This moment, and all moments, do and do not need more. There are thousands of stories in this.

Think about this before asking for more.

This is the truth.

Helpful and Hopeful
Reading 21

In the smallest of motions lies the power of expansion.

Dearest one,

Can you hear us clapping? Your movement using hands to do the work is expansion work. It is one thing to see and to know. It is entirely another to do—one of the smallest word units in human construct—to do.

Please do. Just do. Do. Without do, expansion does not occur. It is mere movement in place. Expansion of thought in human but not in soul expansion.

What to Do with IT? What do you mean IT?

Nothing so expansive can be reduced to two letters while I just told you 'do' was expansion. Ha! The paradox of small/large, action/inaction, specific/general—as we have encouraged expanded thought to include acceptance of micro/macro paradox.

Do = huge! It = reductive unless moved to side of expansive. It = all soul work.

Do. All. Soul. Work.

Such is your life. IT is soul work and should never be reduced to 'only', narrowed to exclude and restrict.

Soul work means to do in all life's arenas and choices—all this living, helpful and hopeful.

There lies the guiding principle of that so large. In the smallest of motions lies the power of expansion. In the cell, in the leaf, in the roots of the tree, in the earth, in the universe with many layers unmentioned in between.

Do. It.

In large proportion some/all phases between the cell—to the universe—to the divine.

It teems with life. You teem with life. Through body you are given hands to sculpt a path to the divine. Expand toward the divine unity we all seek.

You have paused to contemplate the meaning of this, but can you, really?

It can be too big to grasp in brain weighted by ego, muddled by emotion. But even that should not be daunting. The intangible thought becomes the visible work that expands the soul toward love and the divine. Keep it simple. Two letters each.

Do. It.

What? What? What?

Can you not see how that human inquisition serves to expand in this case—human, body, mind, soul working in concert to implement micro to macro. Hands to divine connection.

So, what to do with this?

Do. That is the free will that defines soul's search for expansion. Yes, opportunity is present, but choice guides the journey.

Core question. What do you want to do with it? The possibility is there, the hands are yours to steer the path of your own expansion, so it is fruitless to ask others.

What to do? That is your question alone. Sorry. We can open windows, but you must open doors.

Do it.

Do what?

Your question. Your answer. While we would love to help you out here, it isn't OURS to do.

Tsk. Tsk. Sorry, but not really.

That question and its answer are always yours.

Arrogance and Judgment
Reading 22

Let all trip lightly down their own paths.

Greetings on day of powerful winds and thoughts. Begin
with these questions. What is this? Who are you? What am
I? What am I seeing/hearing here?

Listen deeply. Get ready to hear.

We are talking to you and through you mostly because you
have stood at the window, nose pressed against the glass—
asking—what is this? We have answered this for you in bits
and pieces. Now we will say it straight.

It is a connection we all share. So yes, it is part filtered by
you, based on your experience, but that does not mean other
factors at work.

Yes, it is your imagination—your ability to imagine beyond
the physical embodiment of you currently. Whoever said
imagination is always fictitious? Not based on truth? It
simply means you can take what you have seen, add in what
has stirred you, listen to ideas beyond your perception. Does
that mean they are fake, not based in reality?

We often attribute imagination to children. They are allowed
to see things, feel things, say things outside the rule of the
provable. But adults? No! That has got to stop. Get back
to reality which means what you can see and prove. Even
your feelings are merely tangibles within your control. Sad?
Stop that! Choose happiness. It is up to you, like picking out
a meal or an outfit. Totally up to you.

But why do children have this ability to wander beyond the choice of the matter and formulate wild imaginings without consequence? They—we—are all given that gift. It is a gift given to all in human form, but like with all gifts the use entirely voluntary, so when born into scientific, controllable environment it is crushed. The openness to beyond, the sway of the wild cannot be proven. Tame it all so it can come down to earth and reside in your hands to construct a life that makes perfect sense.

Our child does not go away. Our gifts do not go away. People still long to complete themselves by seeking that which we know to be there but vanished inexplicably into practicality and convention.

Advice to all. Imagine away! Do not fear the tsk tsk of those who wish to raise their brows at your folly.

And DO NOT get arrogant and raise your brows about their choices, either. You are not the judge of anything except your own vision—your construction of the view. Some won't see. Don't see. Struggle to see. See clearly. Skew what they see. That is the only control that humans have, but do not ever confuse seeing with judging—not your role.

Your decision is what to do with your own sight. What are you open to seeing? Shape your own truth of what you see. If you are willing to open your view to original gifts, they become yours to do what you will.

But beware the imprint of your own actions as outgrowth of your own sight. Explore it. Refine it. Use it in heart work. Be totally uninvolved in gift use of others. That is not up to you.

You only lie in judgment of your own hands, not the actions, choices wrought by others. Their perceived 'shortcomings' not for you to record in the annals of time.

Yes, paths may cross. Energies intersect. But these encounters are for enlightenment, not judgment—and you cannot judge the value of any one intersection, especially if your role is as observer.

Let all trip lightly down their own paths.

Even now you are struggling to judge what we are saying while ironically missing entirely what we are saying.

Our energies are currently intersecting for the purpose of enlightenment. Take it only as such, but do not judge it as to its cosmic imprint. It is for you. Does it help you see? Can you use this general ability to help others see? Do not judge others on the basis of their intersection with you. Who knows the purpose of that?

Trip your own path lightly, illuminated beyond what you think we are 'revealing' to you. It is you just looking and saying, "Oh yes, I see that." You must accept this for the reality of all concerned.

It is there. Not everyone sees the same thing. Not everyone should. Your sight is limited, too, so never state the absolute that your sight is reality. It is merely your own gift of imaginative sight.

Oh, so much roil.

Leave it there. No compact little ditty at the end of this reading.

It is a mystery after all. And so are you.

Here's the Thing

Reading 23

The stream becomes what you make of it and nothing more.

Waiting. Waiting. Waiting. Patience for all here and there. All morning we have been talking to which you said, "Wait. Wait. Wait."

Such as it is—messages flowing. You are waiting. What are you waiting for? Quiet mind clutter and listen carefully.

Not—what should I do next? Right question—what should I do now?

To ignore all that we have said is your prerogative, but you keep playing the same tape. Same question. Over and over and over . . ..

What is coming next? Ignore that worry.

Ask. What to do now?

Are you waiting for a sign? A big cosmic nudge? Our quiet voices are not enough?

Today you can live all that we have told you. You can tomorrow as well. Or not. See those balls up in the air and you can keep juggling. What to do with this? What to do with that?

Our message is clear. You feel like something is ending. Now what?

Put all in the stream but look down and see the water as it swirls around your feet. Do not continue to look back, straining to see the things that have rushed past. Or peer into the forward, trying to determine where to go or what to do or what will flow past you next. Stand right here and you have your answer.

The only problem is you fail to accept it and keep those human eyes scanning back and forward searching for an answer that already surrounds you.

Stand still. Frolic in the stream. Paddle about. Fish or splash. Cup water in your hands. Fling it about. Play. Worry it is too cold. Too fast. Too dangerous. In all of it, the stream becomes what you make of it and nothing more.

It will flow no matter what and the only variant is your perception of it. Own the perception as it is the only thing that taps into the power you have. All the actions you take will never alter the flow. Stop analyzing everything we say. Just stand in the stream and absorb.

The human in you is struggling. What! I can't build a dam! I can't control the current? No. The only power of potential you have is to shape it as it flows past you. Stand alone. Invite others to stand by you. The flow is the flow and you are only free to define how your humanness responds to it. You are struggling with this mightily.

You have taken in many lessons that flowed by you, but you did not control that flow. You made many earthly decisions about career and family and life but think deeply. Did that change the stream or were you merely managing (as we have told you) how you felt it go past in life force energy.

Continue to do that, only more deliberately. Keep doing what all humans do, but often refuse to admit or accept. You really aren't the controller of all life around you. Your decision is how to live in the water—live in the energy.

Instead of robbing you of a false control, it gives you all the control—how to respond. How to engage. How to live. So back to question. What's next? Such a good/bad question! Better question. What now?

Answer to that question is entirely up to you!

Even choosing to bobble down the stream or struggle against the flow is up to you. Take control of the power you have and stop wondering what outside forces will guide you next. So much to try to control! So much power given to things you cannot! Not much clarity to this paradox of power.

Heal in. Harness the power of in to live boldly out. In and out—same thread. You can heal the in. You can heal the out. Divine threads of oneness. Overwhelming? Yes! Impossible to grasp and live? No!

Go back to the stream. Ask. What to do with you today? Then stop asking that question if you can. Start to feel the water infuse you with life—then live.

Is this too much for you? Not if you can stop that human tape that keeps asking, what? Shake your fist all you want, but we can't give you an answer we don't have—BUT YOU DO! It isn't our answer. It is yours.

The Magic Answer
Reading 24

A quest does not require a question.

Greetings this morning of sunny days and open mind.

There is a filter running; flip that switch to allow a pure message to enter. We will wait.

The garden, the library all the same. It is us trying to reach you with visions that clarify your understanding of the things beyond the curtain you cannot as human grasp at full understanding. So, there is your answer to today's inquiry— the one you never voiced, but we heard.

How to live there happily, given all the overwhelming problems inherent in doing so?

As the magician you think if you just use the tools, understand them, wield them, you will find some secret key to peace and happiness as a human entity making your way in this time and place.

But you are mistaken in so many ways. Your thoughts are clouded by the very humanity you believe you can overcome with enough diligence, enough practice, enough insight. If you could just pull back that curtain to see the truth of joyous life accessible through spirit. Sorry, no garden gate will open you to full entry and clarity. No guides will give you that answer because there is no answer to give you.

It is a journey and as with all travel it has its discomforts and its revelations. Stop trying to mitigate one to find the other. It is wrong to believe if you just see more you will understand more, then you can control more of your emotions and life circumstances. Yet you have been told it is not a matter of control at all. It is a matter of release and acceptance.

You absolutely know it lies there in heart center. Release control of the journey and yet that struggle remains front and center. How to grasp and maintain the joy that slips through your fingers? How to banish the darkness that haunts you, tapping, tapping on your shoulder when life is happening and no despair is called for?

Paradox. Always paradox. Control/Release. Control/Accept.

The myth persists. If you just do _____, then you will feel _____ and your life will be _____ and you will find the secret to happiness through action and tea leaves.

Again, we say. That is not it.

You live the journey. You don't plan and implement and control all the layers at play. It is so vast—a myriad of factors to assess and control—how you feel, how others feel, when spring ends, the infinite choices made by you and all others and those choices unmade.

I would be happy if _____ and when _____.

Life played as a game only to be considered successful if you are able to maneuver to where exactly you wish to go and even that remains indeterminate. What is the destination you seek?

There you have it. From start to finish, soup to nuts, you have no idea after all and in trying to seek THE answer, you fail to see the ANSWER.

Ha! Even now your mind asks, so what is the ANSWER you just mentioned? There isn't one! The ANSWER is there isn't an answer. Let. That. Go.

Oh, yes. You are on a journey but recognize the layers of complexity and curtains that exist beyond full understanding are not obstacles to overcome to find some answer, the magical answer safely ensconced at the top of some mountain.

You keep saying, feeling, if only I could understand the nature of acceptance and joy, I could make them mine forever. They are mere elements of the complicated journey, so in reality you just need to open your heart wide enough to allow all parts of the journey into your view out the window as life goes by. It is not a matter of mastery or defeat. It is the ability to journey on without selecting the dominate or dwelling in the place of limited sphere.

Do not allow despair to overwhelm you because light is right there beside it. See both. Notice both. Not control both. Don't say, oh, there is despair. I must banish this and feel only light.

No, today despair dwells here while the sun shines there. Getting back to the answerless question.

A quest does not require a question, especially questions that will mire you in a constant quest to find the one, best, right response.

Ponder the idea of release and how that plays into acceptance and how that allows for a more satisfying journey. It is a non-answer. Stop looking for the answer. Release yourself from the drumbeat of why, why, how, when, why . . ..

When despair nestles in your heart, there sits the challenge of the journey. It feels bad and you want an answer, but one is not forthcoming, so you must sit with that in your own space.

Look at all the 'tools' you think you have, then perhaps look at the futility of using them to create a particular outcome that will make all right. Look at them as tools of release rather than tools of accomplishment, tools of creation and expansion, tools of mystery and illusion.

This does not sit easily, but it sits truthfully. No one ever said there was a destination. No one ever said the journey could be turned into nirvana, free from human foibles. You are seeking the elusive and it will forever frustrate you because what you seek does not exist. So, today's message—contemplate all facets of the existence you live and redefine what you are doing while there and give up your beliefs there are actual answers to all questions.

What answers are you hoping to find?

How do I live a happy life how do I learn to fit in how can I find meaning in my endeavors who am I how can I get connections what is the key to understanding life what to do with my gifts what are my gifts how to make life smoother how can I banish despair how do I live with past events how do I have better relationships how do I accept injustice in the world what do I feel why do I feel it will I die happy or unhappy how will the rest of my years go what happens after I die what should I do with my earthly body and possession up death why do I feel responsible for everyone's happiness what am I supposed to be doing what do it want what activities and life choices will make me happy what do it need to do to be a good human how do I live spiritually while human how should I deal with residual traces of former influences why do I do the things I do?

Oh, my. The weight of all this. Release it.

We have told you what you need to know, but please do not call it an answer. We have never given you answers. The magical answers to the infinite questions do not exist.

Every Day Crossroads
Reading 25

The ego tells you to worry about the past and the future.

Beginning/End
Beginning/End

That is how it goes, how it flows. No such start or stop, really.

When you reach the crossroad where the inkling leads you to ending, examine the other footpaths before you. Alas, you cannot see down the roads for insight into best choice.

Stop. Look around. Close your eyes. Listen to your heart. Where should my next footstep be placed? What path can I create if I take this step, then the next and the next . . ..

It looks like predetermined paths exist far off on the horizon, but please know those are your dreams and fears made mirage by your thoughts. They are not a real destination because no such thing as a destination exists—or pathway for that matter.

You are visualizing paths and destinations you imagine. The only certainties that exist are your choices; how you view the end that ends nothing; how you view the future, although it foretells nothing.

It is your feet taking a step that propels you forward and creates the moment of possibility—followed by another— and another—

No real end. No real beginning. Just steps continuing this soul journey of expansion toward love and light.

Choices abound:

Peer backward for answers. Stand still, feet planted in mud.

Peer forward looking for assurances you are headed in the 'right' direction. Stand still.

Feet mired in uncertainty.

Better yet, step deliberately and courageously forward using the power of your authentic self as a guide.

If you listen to your heart, your soul self is there. If you listen to the whispers of authentic soul self, spirit is there to bolster you with confidence in direction.

They are telling you where to put your feet that best fulfills your soul destiny on this journey.

The ego tells you to worry about the past and the future. The soul tells you how to reside at the crossroads and create the next, best possibility in light and love.

ABOUT THE AUTHOR

L.M. Reed is a writer, teacher, mother, seeker, and perennial problem child who has always used words as her tool of choice. Throughout her life, spirit tapped her love of words to explain the puzzling, mysterious and divine concerns beyond human ego eyes. After an Akashic Records workshop, spirit revealed through a series of messages how she could heal her heart to free her spirit. They later suggested she share these insights with others. Currently, she does that as a writer and spiritual consultant for those who want to heal themselves, expand spiritually and lead more authentic, satisfying lives.

ABOUT THE ILLUSTRATOR

Gracie Walsh is an artist, musician, and mother with a healthy interest in what waits for us beyond this world. Using whatever medium best fits the task at hand, she has always been eager to take on projects that resonate on a personal level. The opportunity to illustrate spirit's message through the author has been a thrill in pen-and-ink. While on her current plane of existence, she lives in the Finger Lakes region of New York with her husband, daughter, and spaniel mix, Hugo.

www.ingramcontent.com/pod-product-compliance
Lightning Source LLC
Chambersburg PA
CBHW021924040426
42448CB00008B/897